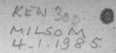

Penguin Education

Penguin Science of Behaviour
General Editor: B. M. Foss

Abnormal and C
Editors: Max Har

The Study of Twins
Peter Mittler

The Study of Twins

Peter Mittler

Penguin Books

Penguin Books Ltd, Harmondsworth,
Middlesex, England
Penguin Books Inc., 7110 Ambassador Road,
Baltimore, Md 21207, U.S.A.
Penguin Books Australia Ltd,
Ringwood, Victoria, Australia

First published 1971
Copyright © Peter Mittler, 1971

Made and printed in Great Britain by
Hazell Watson & Viney Ltd,
Aylesbury, Bucks
Set in Linotype Times

Penguin Science of Behaviour

This book is one of an ambitious project, the Penguin Science of Behaviour, which covers a very wide range of psychological inquiry. Many of the short 'unit' texts are on central teaching topics, while others deal with present theoretical and empirical work which the Editors consider to be important new contributions to psychology. We have kept in mind both the teaching divisions of psychology and also the needs of pyschology at work. For readers working with children, for example, some of the units in the field of Developmental Psychology will deal with psychological techniques in testing children, other units will deal with work on cognitive growth. For academic psychologists, there will be units in well-established areas such as Learning and Perception, but also units which do not fall neatly under one heading, or which are thought of as 'applied', but which nevertheless are highly relevant to psychology as a whole.

The project is published in short units for two main reasons. Firstly, a large range of short texts at inexpensive prices gives the teacher a flexibility in planning his course and recommending texts for it. Secondly, the pace at which important new work is published requires the project to be adaptable. Our plan allows a unit to be revised or a fresh unit to be added with maximum speed and minimal cost to the reader.

Above all, for students, the different viewpoints of many authors, sometimes overlapping, sometimes in contradiction, and the range of topics Editors have selected will reveal the complexity and diversity which exist beyond the necessarily conventional headings of an introductory course.

B.M.F.

Contents

Part Three Overview

Editorial Foreword

The study of twins contributes uniquely to human biology. Since Galton's pioneer work, there has been a small but continuous stream of research in this field. The original naïve notions that such studies would solve the problems of 'nature–nurture' have, like all naïve approaches to biology, been disappointing. Modern refinements in techniques and investigations, however, and – even more importantly – in theoretical concepts, have shown how the study of twins can yield information scarcely obtainable in any other way. The most immediate and practical value lies in the study of genetic factors of disease, especially in the context of mental disease. The studies on cognitive development and on personality are of more theoretical interest but nonetheless important.

Dr Mittler is to be congratulated on bringing together and making easily accessible so much material. Whatever the interest of the reader, whether it be in particular problems of human psychology or in abnormal behaviour, he will gain much from this book.

M.H.

Preface

About twelve years ago, I was asked to see a pair of speechless, overactive and rather wild four-year-old twin boys whose mother was near breaking point. Their intellectual functioning at that time was for all practical purposes subnormal, and their tested IQs were in the low 60s. We merely advised the mother that she should treat each child as an individual, dress them differently, call them by their own names rather than refer to them collectively as 'the twins', and in general do everything possible to stress the individuality of each child. A year later, for whatever reason, their IQs had risen to around 120, they were speaking fluently and their behaviour was normal. They continued to score well above average on intelligence tests throughout their school careers. After that, I came across a number of other pairs, some of whom were seriously disturbed or psychotic, while others showed a variety of learning problems. In all cases, the quality of the relationship between the twins seemed to change continuously, so that mothers found it hard to describe one twin as consistently more dominant or more affectionate than the other.

When I began to read the voluminous literature on twins, it became clear to me that many variables relating to twins and the twin situation were still unexplored, and that psychologists who used twins as pawns in the nature–nurture controversy were concentrating exclusively on differences within pairs and neglecting both the twin as an individual and the psychology of the twin pair. What factors, for example, could be related to the fact that twins tend to show delayed language development? Was it because they tend to form a closed communication unit and to develop a private language? Or could it be because they tended also to be prematurely born and to have low birth weights? It was questions of this kind that led me to realize that the study of twins as individuals might contribute to an understanding of the interactions between biological and social factors in development.

My indebtedness to many workers in this field will be obvious. The works of Professor Luria and Professor Zazzo were among the first to influence my thinking, and many others have followed. Unfortunately *The Biology of Twinning in Man* by M. G. Bulmer* and 'Heredity and psychological abnormality' by J. Shields† appeared after this book was passed for press. In writing this review of twin studies, I have been greatly helped by Professors Vandenberg, Eysenck and Jensen, and by Mr James Shields, though responsibility for errors of emphasis or fact is mine alone. I am grateful to Sybil Shields, Carol Tansley and Alyce Sandes for secretarial help. My greatest debt is to my wife, who has listened patiently and criticized constructively throughout the book's prolonged gestation.

*Oxford University Press, 1970.

† In H. J. Eysenck (ed.), *Handbook of Abnormal Psychology*, Pitman, 1971.

Acknowledgements

Acknowledgement is made to the following publishers and journals for permission to reprint copyright material. The source of each figure, table or extract is given in the text, and the publisher or journal in the references.

Acta Psychiatrica Scandinavia; *American Journal of Psychiatry*; *British Journal of Psychology*; Chapman & Hall; Churchill; *Harvard Educational Review*; Johns Hopkins Press; *Journal of Child Psychology and Child Psychiatry*; *Journal of Mental Science*; *Journal of Psychiatric Research*; McGraw-Hill; *Merrill Palmer Quarterly*; *Multivarate Behavior Research*; National Academy of Sciences; Oliver & Boyd; Oxford University Press; *Perceptual Motor Skills*; Presses Universitaires de France; *Psychology Bulletin*; Routledge & Kegan Paul; Russell Sage Foundation; *Science*; C. C. Thomas; University of Chicago Press; Wiley.

Glossary of Genetic Terms

allele one of two or more forms of a gene occupying a particular locus

chromosome one of twenty-three paired stringlike substances in the nucleus of each cell, visible during a stage of cell division, consisting of a very long protein molecule

cytoplasm protoplasm surrounding the nucleus of a cell

dizygotic (DZ, dizygous, binovular, fraternal) twins arising from two fertilized eggs. May be same-sexed or opposite sex pairs

dominant a trait is called dominant if in a certain environment the heterozygote shows that trait, thus 'hiding' the other allele which is called 'recessive'

Down's Syndrome (mongolism) individuals with twenty-one trisomy or translocation of excess part of twenty-one chromosome to other chromosomes

gamete a mature sex cell (egg or sperm)

gene unit of heredity located somewhere on chromosome

genotype the entire genetic complement of an individual

heterozygous condition in which members of a pair of genes are in different allelic form

homozygous condition in which both members of a pair of genes are in the same allelic form

locus position on a chromosome occupied by allelic forms of a given gene

mitosis process by which nuclei resulting from cell division are provided with full chromosomal complements

monozygotic (MZ, monozygous, monovular, uniovular, identical) twins arising from a single fertilized egg. Always same sex

mutation alteration in hereditary material

phenotype observable or measurable characteristic

sex chromosomes chromosomes particularly involved in sex determination; in man, females have two homologous X chromosomes, males have one X and one non-homologous Y chromosome

translocation fault in cell division such that one chromosome acquires extra section while other loses it

zygote the cell produced by union of gametes

Source: McLean (1964); Vandenberg (1969a).

Introduction

Why twin studies? The answers to this question are complex, but it is one of the aims of this book to suggest some of them. Briefly, we might say that the current twin revival is less concerned with the heredity–environment issue as formerly understood, but has been broadened and redefined as an interest in the interaction between biological and social aspects of behaviour and development. Although we have probably made only a little progress so far in understanding these determinants of human development, the questions raised are obviously of fundamental importance.

Twin studies can contribute to these attempts, partly because we are learning to ask better questions, and partly because we are refining our techniques of tackling them. Recent twin studies in the sphere of cognitive skills, for example, are less concerned with global intelligence than with attempts to understand not only the extent, but also the nature of the genetic contribution to specific intellectual abilities. In other words, we have begun to refine our terms. We no longer ask whether 'personality is inherited', but try to assess, admittedly with imperfect tests, whether some aspects of personality appear to be more strongly affected by heredity than others. We also try to speak of 'environment' not as an amorphous and rather nebulous set of forces, but as a series of specific variables, some of which can be isolated, identified and measured with some degree of precision.

In addition, technical and methodological advances have provided us with powerful tools, particularly the computer. We can now study some of the physiological correlates of behaviour by the use of EEG and evoked potential techniques and try to identify genetic components at increasingly molecular levels of behaviour. Our twin subjects are likely to be studied at an earlier stage; psychologists have in recent years discovered rich fields for research in the newborn baby and the very young child, and learned that the neonate is already equipped with surprisingly mature perceptual skills. Complex methods for studying the behaviour of newborns have been developed, and these will in all probability be used with twins who have until now been studied by psychologists only when they were able to tackle intelligence tests. The advantage of studying newborn twins is obvious, even though they have already been subjected to 'environmental' influences for nine months *in utero*.

Considerable advances can also be expected from the development of more sophisticated statistical techniques for the analysis of data derived not only from twins but from family and pedigree studies. In particular, multivariate methods of analysis and the use of specially prepared computer programs will enable large quantities of material to be analysed with the complexity which the subject undoubtedly deserves. Some of the older twin studies are already being re-analysed by means of modern biometric techniques derived from quantitative genetics; one of the happier results of such collaboration is that geneticists and psychologists who once had so many interests in common will again learn to combine their skills in the design of new investigations.

This book will try to provide a framework within which the reader can critically evaluate the many studies which have been conducted on twins. A short book, such as this, cannot cover exhaustively such an extensive literature, but even a limited review of some of the more important studies can contribute to a critical appraisal of the assets and deficits of the twin method. Such a framework should prove useful in considering current and future trends.

It is important to stress at the outset that headings such as 'perception', 'intelligence', 'personality', 'psychosis' are merely convenient for the purpose of classifying wealth of material available. Psychologists are tending to blur some of the conventional distinctions between, for example, sensation and perception, perception and intelligence, intelligence and personality. Moreover, each of these global constructs, and many others such as 'language', 'learning' and 'memory' can be broken down into constituent processes rather than continue to be treated as simple entities. This consideration is relevant for twin studies because we are beginning to find that when cognitive processes are considered as specific abilities rather than in terms of an overall intelligence quotient, genetic factors appear to play a more important part in some abilities than in others. This is one of the directions which research appears to be taking, but twin studies are here dependent on developments in educational psychology and test construction; tests of specific abilities have not yet been shown to be sufficiently reliable or, indeed, sufficiently independent to be confidently used in genetic investigations. Nevertheless, they can provide a provisional rank order within a battery of tests such as the Primary Mental Abilities or the Illinois Test of Psycholinguistic Abilities.

It may be objected that this book over-emphasizes the individuality of twins, and stresses that in many respects they are not fully representative of the population as a whole. But it is only comparatively recently – in fact only since the time of Galton – that scientists have become preoccupied with studying twins in pairs. Long before this, twins have had a fascination of their own, and were regarded in many societies as 'unique' people to be venerated or feared for their special qualities. There is no reason to doubt that some vestige of these attitudes persists among mothers of twins and also in the general public. At the very least the arrival of twins is regarded as a special event, if only as the occasion for ribald comment. The first chapter provides a brief introduction to anthropological and historical material on twins, while the second elaborates in greater detail on the differences between twins and singletons, especially in respect of intellectual, educational and biological variables;

attention is also devoted to the specific question of attitudes to twins, because these are possible sources of bias in research studies.

Chapter 3 deals in some detail with 'the twin method' in psychology, and attempts a critical evaluation of its basic assumptions, and also its advantages and disadvantages. The remainder of the book is devoted to an examination of research findings.

The book as a whole contains three clusters of aims: first, a survey of twin studies; secondly, a consideration of the contribution of twin studies to the 'nature–nurture' question; thirdly, an attempt to relate twin studies and their implications to current concepts in psychology and the developmental sciences.

Part One **Background**

1 From Mythology to Science

Man's preoccupation with the twin phenomenon stretches far back into mythology, partly perhaps because twins provide in miniature a model of man's evolutionary development, embracing his search for identity both as an individual and as a member of society. The need for survival drove him into small bands, whose members were united by their immediate biological needs, and then into ever more complex forms of social organization and relationships. Life in such communities increasingly demanded both an understanding of oneself and an ability to live with others. It is this dialectic which finds its clearest expression in the twin situation.

Twins in mythology and literature

Twins have been the objects of fascinated interest in most societies. From the earliest times there are records testifying to their rarity and often to their special powers for both good and ill. They have been credited with the ability to control the elements, to confer sterility, fertility and immortality in battle. Mythology and primitive religions include many examples of twin deities, sometimes representing polarities of human experience in life and death, and good and evil. In Indian mythology the twin gods Asvin were credited with miracles such as rejuvenating the old, healing the sick and removing the curse of infertility. The American Indian myths also contain many examples of the special relationship of twins to each other, and tell how the death of one was always followed by the death of the other, either naturally or because the surviving twin allows himself to be killed in battle.

Although twins and twin gods were usually regarded as the agents of miracles in mythology and religion, the anthropological evidence reveals that the birth of twins has not always been regarded so favourably. Gedda (1961) quotes examples from Australasia, Japan and India where the mother of twins was ostracized and regarded as impure, perhaps because a double birth was sometimes regarded as proof of infidelity in monogamous societies. It was not uncommon for one or both twins to be left to die, or to be ceremonially killed, while the Hottentots were so frightened of the possibility of a further twin birth that they removed one of the father's testicles. Among some North-American Indian tribes, the female of opposite sex pairs was suffocated, because of the risk of incest in later life, and even because the incest was thought possibly to have occurred before birth. There are also reports of infanticide of the second born twin because he was believed not to be a 'real person', or, more realistically perhaps, because the economic burden of looking after two children was too great. Nevertheless, although the birth of twins has been regarded as a favourable omen by most societies, and they have been treated as special individuals to be venerated and respected, an element of ambivalence may survive in our own attitudes.

In literature, most of the earlier stories concentrate on the obvious device of mistaken identity, especially in Shakespeare, himself the father of twins, but in 1848 George Sand's novel *La Petite Fadette* foreshadowed later psychological thinking by introducing a character who allays the parents' fears of too close a relationship between their twins by advising them on all accounts to treat them as two individuals, stressing their differences more than their similarities. Thornton Wilder's *The Bridge of San Luis Rey* (1941) also refers to the 'secret language' which is commonly reported between twins (Zazzo, 1960).

Medical and scientific studies

By comparison with the evidence from mythology, anthropology and literature, the scientific study of twins is a comparatively recent phenomenon. Early Greek writers, such as Hippocrates, Galen and Empedocles discusssed the origins of twin conceptions, in relation to congenital malformations and the birth of monstrosities. According to Gedda (1961) who provides the best historical account of the subject, Hippocrates believed that twins were conceived by the division of the sperm into two parts, and other writers indulged in similar speculations. No scientific studies appear to have been carried out until the Renaissance, when interest focused on precise anatomical descriptions and on the mechanical hazards of delivery. Gedda (1961) reproduces an authentic wax representation of a pregnant uterus containing dichorial twins, and adds that these reflect an accurate knowledge of ovular membranes. Nevertheless, the birth of twins continued for many years to be an object of astrological inquiry.

Serious scientific investigations are generally regarded as dating from the work of Sir Francis Galton, whose paper *The History of Twins as a Criterion of the Relative Powers of Nature and Nurture* (1875) and his classic *Inquiries into Human Faculty and Its Development* (1883) formed the starting point for most modern researches. Galton clearly foresaw the usefulness as well as most of the difficulties of the twin method in the study of genetic factors in behaviour. He was the first to realize that identical (or monozygotic) twins probably resulted from the splitting of a single fertilized ovum, while fraternal (or dizygotic) twins resulted from the fertilization of two separate ova. Most of the early evidence which he reported was based on correspondence with thirty-five pairs who were probably identical; and another twenty who were probably fraternal; his discussion concentrates on physical characteristics such as appearance, and on concordance in illnesses, including psychosis. His discussion of the fraternal pairs is more sketchy, but did establish that they were no more alike than ordinary siblings, and that they did not grow more alike as a result of

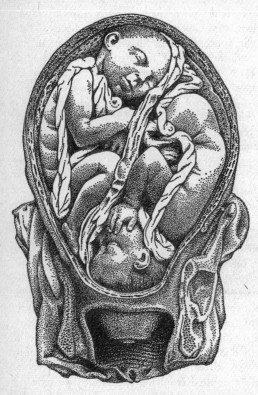

Figure 1 Pregnant uterus containing dichorial twins and opened anteriorly, prepared in wax by the sculptor, G. B. Manfredini; the original was provided by the anatomist, Carlo Mondini of Bologna (c. 1779)

sharing the same environment. He found 'differences of disposition' even in his identical pairs, but attributed these to serious illness or accident.

The first scientific study to make use of tests was that of

Thorndike (1905). He used a mixed battery of 'intelligence' and attainment tests, including tests deliberately designed to measure formal training, such as addition and multiplication, and others which, he assumed, were less affected by formal training, such as word opposites, misspellings and serial cancellation tasks. He found that within pair correlations were the same for 'trained' as for 'untrained' functions, and therefore concluded that 'the similarity of twins was inherent rather than acquired'. This conclusion was reinforced by a second finding that the correlations for older twins were slightly lower than those for younger twins; Thorndike argued that if environmental factors were important in creating similarity, they should become greater as the child became older.

The first study which systematically compared twins with other children was that of Merriman (1924) who used the 1916 version of the Stanford–Binet Scale, as well as the Army Beta and the National Intelligence Scale, and also collected teachers' estimates of intelligence. Although he was mainly concerned with comparison of identical and fraternal twins, he also tabulated the distribution of IQs of the entire group of twins. The mean IQ of his twin groups was only ninety-six but he concluded that twins suffered no intellectual handicap, and attributed the lower mean score to selection effects.

Following these early studies, twin research was conducted intensively in many countries. This will be reviewed in later chapters, but it is important to stress that many disciplines other than psychology make use of the twin method; in particular, epidemiological studies of health and morbidity have made an important contribution to medical knowledge. The World Health Organization (1966) has published a register of twin studies from which it is clear that twin research is actively carried out in many countries, especially the USA, the Scandinavian countries and Japan. The many topics listed by WHO range from alcoholism to rheumatic diseases. Much research is now devoted to refining measures of zygosity determination, and to the variations in twinning rates in different parts of the world. The increased likelihood of multiple birth following hormone therapy for infertility is also the focus of much scientific work at the present time and will increase the number of triplets and quadruplets available for study.

2 Twins as Individuals

Until recently, twins have been used as pawns in the nature-nurture controversy to the neglect of more serious study of their individual psychological characteristics, or, with few exceptions, of the psychology of the twin pair. The few studies which have considered twins as individuals rather than as members of a pair have consistently indicated that they are anything but a typical sample of the population either biologically, intellectually or educationally. Before considering the contribution of twin studies to our knowledge of human behaviour genetics, we must obviously consider the justification, both logical and psychological, of attempts to estimate the contribution of genetic factors in the normal population from studies based on samples of twins who may be atypical in respect of the characteristic being studied.

Intellectual differences

Although most studies concentrate on comparisons of identical and fraternal pairs (Erlenmeyer-Kimling and Jarvik, 1963), very few have compared the mean scores of twins with those that might be expected in the general population. Evidence from several studies, however, indicates that twins achieve below average scores on intelligence tests.

Merriman (1924), Wingfield (1928) and Lauterbach (1925) all reported IQs of around ninety-five on the 1916 version of the Stanford–Binet test, but three important studies will now be more fully discussed; the Scottish mental survey (Scottish Council for Research in Education, 1953), the French national study (Zazzo, 1960) and Koch's (1966) study of ninety-six five- and six-year-old twin pairs in Chicago.

The Scottish mental survey

The Scottish mental survey of the intelligence of all Scottish eleven-year-old children in 1947 was a sequel to a survey carried out in 1932 on a similar population (Scottish Council for Research in Education, 1939, 1949, 1953). The 1947 survey covered 75,000 pupils, of whom some 7400 were intensively investigated, not only with group intelligence tests, but by means of individual administration of the Stanford–Binet Test; a great deal of information was also collected on the social composition and family structure of the smaller sample.

The Scottish survey, comparing 974 individual twin children with nearly 70,000 singletons of the same age, showed that the twins' score was on average the equivalent of five points below that of the singletons. However, there was no evidence of an excess of twins with very low scores, nor were there any significant differences in the size of the standard deviations of the twins and non-twins. It was also found that although girls showed higher scores than boys in the larger sample of normal children, the difference in favour of girls was much more marked among the twins. It was tentatively concluded that this difference might be a reflection of the greater vulnerability of the male to birth complications. It is worth noting that this association has since been more strongly confirmed in later studies (Drillien, 1964; Zazzo, 1960; Koch, 1966). The authors also make detailed comparisons between twins and singletons on a variety of social variables, but conclude that 'the original difference of about four to five IQ points between twins and non-twins has not been accounted for in terms of possible differences of age, family structure or environment'. Although age, size of family, age of mother, overcrowding in the home and socio-economic status of the parents were all correlated with the intelligence test scores of both twins and non-twins, the twins remained at a constantly lower level than the singletons. Their final, somewhat vague conclusion, but one which is shared by other investigators, is that the 'intellectual inferiority of twins ... is probably due to factors inherent in twinning as such' (Scottish Council for Research in Education, 1953, p. 157).

The French national study

This comparatively little known but large-scale study used data from a wider national study of some 100,000 school-children between the ages of six and thirteen years carried out in France in 1944. Zazzo (1960) examined the files of some 800 twins for whom scores on the Gille test were available. According to his description of this test, it appears to measure verbal reasoning. With one exception, all the zygosity and all the age groups obtained median and mean IQ values well below the norm for the entire group of 100,000 children. The means for all same-sexed twins was ninety-two and a half, and that for the opposite sex twins was ninety-four. Differences for older twins (age eleven) compared to matched singletons were no less than for the younger twins. It appears, therefore, that the relative intellectual inferiority of twins is constant up to the age of at least eleven years, whereas it might have been predicted that twins would in some way make up for their initial intellectual inferiority on entering school.

Analysis by seven socio-economic groups showed that twins lagged consistently and almost equally behind the singletons at each of the seven social class levels. The retardation relative to singletons is the same at each social class level – a finding of considerable importance, paralleled in Koch's study (1966) and in Mittler (1970c) but documented for the largest sample and in the greatest detail by Zazzo.

Figure 2 illustrates the manner in which the twin curve follows the slope of the singleton curve almost exactly, but at a substantially lower level (Zazzo 1960, vol. 2, p. 329).

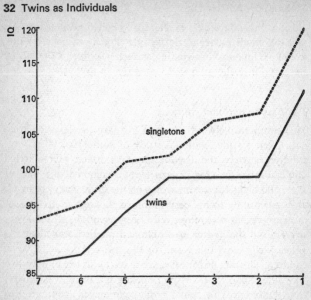

Figure 2 IQ distribution of singletons and twins by social class (adapted from Zazzo, 1960, p. 329)

The Chicago study

The interest of Koch's study (1966) lies not so much in its numbers (which total ninety-six pairs of twins between five and six years old) but in its more analytical approach to 'intelligence'. Instead of a global definition of intelligence in terms of an IQ result, Koch used the Thurstone Primary Abilities Test (PMA) in order to carry out a separate analysis of different intellectual skills – verbal (V), perceptual (P), quantitative (Q), motor (M) and spatial (S).

Koch's analyses are a reflection of the complexity of the interaction between zygosity, social class and sex variables which is found when making comparisons between twins and singletons. She found that although the total PMA did not significantly differentiate the twins from the matched singletons, (except in the case of the MZ boys) all but one of the factors (i.e. V, M, Q and S) showed significantly lower scores for twins than singletons for all sex and zygosity sub-groups, with the exception of the opposite sex (DZOS) pairs. It is of particular interest however, that all the twin groups produced above average scores on the perceptual tests compared to the singletons, whereas the reverse was true for the other factors and especially for the verbal factors. The MZ twins had particularly low scores on the V factor (Koch, 1966).

The studies that have been described in some detail demonstrate the consistent, though relatively slight, tendency for twins to show lower scores on verbal intelligence tests than singleton children. The effects appear to be very similar at each socio-economic level, and differences within different groups of twins have not been consistently established, though it is possible that identical twins are relatively more retarded than fraternals, especially on verbal tests.

A very recent study by Record, McKeown and Edwards (1970) provides further important evidence. They examined the records of all twins taking the 11+ examination in Birmingham in the period 1950–57, and found that the mean verbal reasoning scores of 2164 twins was 95·7, compared to 100·1 for just under 49,000 singletons. These figures must overestimate the scores for the total population, since only those who actually took the 11+ examination were included in the calculations. Their second finding is of even greater interest: in view of the large and representative sample to which they had access, they were able to compare twins brought up together with those whose twin was still-born or had died within a short period. The mean IQ of 148 twin survivors was 98·8 – i.e. only marginally below that of the singletons. The fact that the birth weight of these survivors was the same as that of other twins suggests that the lower IQ scores of twins brought up together must be related to post-natal rather than pre-natal factors, and may again have something to do with 'the twin situation', as suggested by the Scottish surveys.

Educational differences

Educational attainment, as assessed by standardized tests of reading, comprehension, arithmetic, etc., have been less often administered than the conventional intelligence tests, and even when they have been used, the interest has been in intraclass correlations. It is usually assumed that intelligence and attainment tests are highly correlated in normal samples, mainly because they both depend on verbal proficiency to such an extent that it has even been stated that intelligence tests are no more than a form of attainment test (Vernon, 1960). It is important, however, not to blur the differences between the tests, and it is relevant to point out that it is twin studies which have drawn attention to them. The few studies which have compared correlations between intelligence and attainment tests for twins have consistently suggested that genetic and environmental variables operate differentially on intelligence and attainment tests. The two main groups of studies are those of Burt and his associates (summarized in Burt, 1966) and those of Newman, Freeman and Holzinger (1937). Both show that correlations in attainment scores for fraternal twins and for siblings are very high (0·83 and 0·80 in Burt's series) whereas the correlations in attainment tests for identical twins reared apart were only 0·62. These 'attainment' correlations are, of course, quite different from those found in the case of intelligence tests, and indicate, as Burt emphasizes, that the influence of environment appears to be relatively much greater in the case of attainment than in intelligence tests.

Two other studies have dealt specifically with twins' achievement test results. The first was a large scale study by Sandon (1957, 1959) which showed that the likelihood of a twin winning a scholarship award to a grammar school in the eleven-plus secondary school selection examinations was significantly less than that of singletons. The second group of studies are those by Husén (1961, 1963) who conducted a downward extension of his studies on military conscripts by examining achievement test results of 689 pairs of twins who were tested as part of a national programme of achievement testing throughout the whole of Sweden during 1959. Mean scores for twins were significantly below the means for non-twins on reading, writing and arithmetic tests.

Examination of the distribution of test scores led Husén to the conclusion that the lower means among twins were due not only to a higher frequency of low scores, as suggested, for example, by his previous studies (1953), but also to a correspondingly lower frequency of high scores.

Language

The first systematic study of language abilities in young twins was reported by Day (1932); she used a series of *ad hoc* language tests, relying on the pioneer studies of Dorothea McCarthy (1930) – chiefly mean length of response, ratings of grammatical complexity and measures of egocentric and socialized speech (based on Piaget, 1926). Her study demonstrated a clear and striking inferiority of twins compared to singleton controls. Twins showed an overall poverty and reduction of vocabulary, used more immature and primitive sentence constructions and showed a more limited range of those parts of speech which contribute to cognitive operations involving classification, abstraction and conceptualization. Moreover, Day showed that their inferiority on language tests was relatively much greater than that shown on tests of general intelligence, and that their linguistic inferiority increased rather than decreased between two and five years of age. Similar findings were reported by Koch (1966) on the verbal sections of the Primary Mental Abilities tests.

Davis (1937), who extended the earlier study by Day, found that twins approximate more closely to normal language development as they become older, though it is difficult to distinguish the effect of age from that of exposure to school.

A recent study by the writer (Mittler, 1969a, 1970c) compared the performance of 200 four-year-old twins and 100 singleton controls on the Illinois Test of Psycholinguistic Abilities. This test is based on a communication model of Osgood's (1957) and includes nine sub-tests, each purporting to measure a distinct aspect of psycholinguistic functioning. The test distinguishes between channels of communication (e.g. auditory input and vocal output), levels of organization (representational or automatic-sequential) and psycholinguistic processes (decoding, association and encoding).

The performance of the twins was significantly inferior to that of the controls, the retardation corresponding to about six months of language development. Their low scores were seen not only in the ITPA total, but more or less equally over all the nine sub-tests of the scale. Thus, the study suggested that twins do not show any characteristic pattern or profile of psycholinguistic functioning, and that their performance can be best described in terms of an overall immaturity of language development. Identical and fraternal twins showed similar patterns, and were not significantly different from each other. This is in contrast to what one might have predicted, namely, that identical twins would show lower scores than fraternals, partly because they tend to form more of a 'closed communication system' sometimes with a 'secret language', and also because they are more vulnerable to abnormalities of pregnancy, delivery and early development.

Luria and Yudovitch (1959), adopting the theoretical position of Vigotsky (1962), argued that their retardation was due to 'the twin situation', in which neither twin is 'faced with an objective necessity for transition to speech communication, because their lives are linked in the closest possible way, and they understand each other in the course of joint, practical activity' (p. 29). He therefore predicted that merely separating the twins would lead to an acceleration of language development, because each twin would then be constrained to communicate with others in his group. Although the results appear to confirm his prediction, it is unfortunate that separation was quickly followed by a regime of special training given to the less developed of the pair, so that it is difficult to know, in spite of the detailed results which Luria and Yudovitch provide of the language development of both twins, to what extent the improvements can be ascribed to the separation or to the training.

A variety of interpretations have been offered for the language difficulties shown by twins. Biological explanations emphasize the complications of pregnancy and delivery, particularly low birth weight; in singleton children these reproductive complications have been shown to be associated with a higher risk of developmental disorders, including language delays and lower scores on intelligence tests until at least the age of eight (Drillien, 1964; de Hirsch, Jansky and Langford, 1964). However, it cannot be assumed that the long-term significance of a reproductive disorder such as low birth weight is necessarily of the same order for a twin as for a singleton. In our study, biological variables showed only a weak association with language skills at the age of four. Even birth weight did not appear to play as important a part as might have been expected, though low language scores were certainly more commonly found among twins with low birth weight. On the other hand, complications of pregnancy and delivery had no effect on ITPA scores.

Reference has already been made to Luria and Yudovitch's view that the language retardation could be attributed to a reduced need to communicate with others. Psychoanalytic writers such as Burlingham (1952) suggest that each twin has a particularly difficult problem of differentiating his own ego (and body image) from that of his co-twin. Thus, the normal process of differentiating the ego from that of the mother is complicated by the secondary need to achieve a comparable autonomy in respect of one's twin. Twins are not only more isolated by virtue of their close relationship to each other, but also they tend to be born to older mothers, who may already have a large family, making it more difficult for her to spend as much time with them: on this argument, she is more likely to be content to let them play together for long periods.

Little direct evidence can be collected to support such theories. On the psychoanalytic argument, it might be expected that identical twins would be more vulnerable than fraternals, and opposite sex twins to show the fewest difficulties. This was not found in the writer's study. The age of the mother and the number of siblings did not appear to be a significant variable for the twins, though it is interesting that these variables were significant for the singleton controls. Similarly, the effect of social class on language scores was very marked for singletons, though somewhat less obvious for twins.

We must conclude, therefore, that no compelling explanation has yet been advanced to account for the intellectual and linguistic inferiority shown by twins. Most writers fall back lamely on the concept of 'the twin situation' (Zazzo, 1960), or on that of a 'lingering physiological immaturity'.

Biological differences

Intellectual inferiority may be related to more basic biological impairments which again set twins apart from singletons.

In the first place, twins are a comparative biological rarity – one in eighty births in Britain, but as high as one in twenty-two in Nigeria and as low as one in 160 in Japan (Gedda, 1961). They undergo a hazardous pre-natal life, and are considerably more vulnerable as individuals to the development of handicapping conditions in later life. Their embryonic and foetal development is fraught with considerable risks, some of them of a general nature which might occur in any pregnancy – especially toxaemia of pregnancy – others specific to twin pregnancy, such as foetal crowding, or unequal distribution of blood supply due to the 'placental transfusion syndrome' (Strong and Corney, 1967). Their gestation period is shorter by an average of some three weeks than that found in singletons, and their birth weight is about two pounds lower. About fifty-five per cent of twin births are premature by weight, by the internationally agreed criterion of a birth weight of five and a half pounds or under. There are also serious difficulties of delivery; over a third are 'breech' presentations, compared with three per cent of singletons, and the risk to the second-born twin is particularly great. One in six of all multiple pregnancies in England ends in the death of one or both twins (Dunn, 1965).

There is also evidence that a 'growth retardation factor' persists into childhood. It might have been expected that twins would compensate for their low birth weight and growth retardation in later childhood, but it appears from longitudinal studies that this is not, in general, the case (Drillien, 1964). Twins are as a group well below the national norms in both height and weight and in other physical measurements. Drillien's Edinburgh survey (1964) showed that they remained below national norms for height and weight at the age of five years; similar results were obtained by Koch (1966) in Chicago, while Husén (1959) reported that Swedish twins being conscripted for military service still showed significant retardation in height and weight at the age of eighteen years. In his large and representative sample of 873 Swedish young male twins, Husén reported a mean height of 1·3 cm. below the mean of the singleton conscripts, with MZ twins being significantly shorter than DZs; a similar retardation was also found for weight.

The significance of the continued growth retardation of twins goes beyond that of physical development alone. Correlations between height and intelligence test scores have been reported in several investigations – as high as 0·4 in Bayley's study (1956).

Attitudes to twins

Because twins have throughout history been regarded as 'different' by their fellow men, it is reasonable to speculate about the attitudes and child rearing practices of the mothers of the twins themselves, and the effects that such attitudes might have on their behaviour and development. While people in general tend to treat twins as a pair, the mother should be more likely to see differences rather than similarities, and to be responsive to the personality and specific needs of each child. This point is relevant in view of the common assumption that 'the environment of each twin may be regarded as constant'. This may not apply to the subtler aspects of the mother–child relationship, which have so far eluded the researcher. Mothers are usually very articulate about the differences in personality and temperament even within identical pairs, and spontaneously emphasize that each one needs to be treated differently.

It is likely that the mother's attitudes to her twin children will in some respects be different from those that she shows to her other children. This is not to argue that they will necessarily be more positive or negative, 'accepting' or 'rejecting' in the vague way in which these terms are commonly used, but that they are likely to be more complex, if only for the reason that having and rearing twins calls for different 'coping styles'. At the earliest stages, the diagnosis of a twin pregnancy may or may not be a shock, but certainly requires adjustment. Many mothers in our own study, when asked about their reactions on first hearing that they were having twins, reported initial feelings of shock and despair. In some cases this was related to the fact that the pregnancy was itself unplanned, or that two or more children would involve the family in great economic hardship. In other cases, and especially with young mothers, they are likely to be preoccupied with the practical difficulties of managing two infants when they are not yet confident of their ability to handle one.

Over and above these considerations, the question of attitudes may be considered in the theoretical framework of attachment behaviour. Although the attachment behaviour model stems directly from ethological animal studies (especially those of Harlow, 1963) and cannot easily be shown to be directly applicable to man, Ambrose (1961), Bowlby (1957) and others have argued for the relevance of the concept in mother–child interaction, especially in the earliest weeks after birth. In the case of animals, Bowlby (1957) has characterized attachment behaviour as consisting of sucking, clinging and following. The human baby exhibits certain behaviours over and above sucking which appear, according to these theorists, to fulfil the same functions of attaching the mother to the child, and thereby ensuring that he receives care and attention from her. The birth cry, for example, although having the primarily physiological purpose of filling the lungs with oxygen, also serves as a 'helplessness signal' to the mother. Similarly, the baby's reflex grasp of his mother's finger, his fixed stare when feeding, and, at the age of four to six weeks, his first social smile all combine, by emphasizing his helplessness, to ensure the continuation of the mother's care.

Whether or not we accept this model of early mother–infant interaction, it is likely that the birth and mere existence of two infants may bring about psychological reactions that are either qualitatively or quantitatively different from those that may operate in the more normal event of a single birth. Just as 'the human uterus is adapted for the satisfactory gestation of but one infant at a time' (Newman, 1923), it is not unreasonable to conjecture that adjustment to the birth of twins is likely to be of a different order. It is surprising, therefore, to find no studies of maternal attitudes to newborn twins, even though 'attitudes to pregnancy' and similar scales have been developed (e.g. Blau, Welkowitz and Cohen, 1964). In fact, there are very few psychological or behavioural studies of infant twins, in contrast to the large obstetric and paediatric literature on the subject. It seems that the fascination that twins have for psychologists does not begin until their intellectual abilities can be assessed. But newborn twins afford ideal subjects for the study of the heredity and environment issue, since it is obvious that the earlier the age at which twins are studied, the shorter is the period during which environmental variables operate – at least those of a social or cultural nature.

The cultural norm towards twins at the present time appears to be broadly positive, but also has the effect of encouraging mothers to 'display' twins by emphasizing their twinship. Most twins of the same sex tend not only to be dressed alike but also to be called in rhyming or alliterative names. In general, the norm is to emphasize similarities rather than differences. From the psychological point of view, it is pertinent to express certain reservations about this norm, as some psychoanalysts have done, though evidence on this matter is totally absent. The basis of their doubt, echoed in quite a different context by Luria and Yudovitch (1959), is that each twin is less likely to be able to develop a separate 'identity' ('ego boundaries', 'body image', etc.) if he finds himself confronted at every turn by a mirror image of himself. The distinction between 'self' and 'not self' is basic not only to the development of satisfactory body image boundaries and personality (in a general sense of the word) but also has certain cognitive implications; the ability to see the world both perceptually and conceptually from the point of view of another individual is one of the landmarks of Piaget's developmental theory (Piaget, 1951; Flavell, 1963).

Popular books on 'twin-rearing', addressed mainly to parents, are divided on the subject of dressing twins alike, but at least in the United States, where 'twin clubs' now flourish in most of the larger cities, the view appears to be gaining ground that it is better to emphasize the individuality of each twin and to avoid any child-rearing practices which may make for a 'twin unit'; advice is now more frequently along the lines of dressing each child differently, calling each by name rather than referring to both collectively as 'the twins', and in general doing everything possible to encourage each child to follow his own interests and inclinations. As far as is known, no such books (or clubs) exist in Britain, though Scheinfeld's book *Twins and Super Twins* (1968) may become popular, and Dr Spock's best-selling *Baby and Child Care* (1946) has always contained a paragraph on the importance of treating each twin as an individual and avoiding comparisons and jokes about the difficulty of distinguishing between them (p. 765).

It is also relevant to stress that whatever the mother's attitudes may be in these matters, they may not be shared by other members of the family, or by adults and children with whom the twins come into contact. Several recent studies attest to the popularity of twins in school. Pire (1966) reports a sociometric study from France which shows not only that adolescent twins are relatively more popular among their classmates than non-twins, but that they are nearly always chosen in pairs – i.e. if one twin is chosen to be a member of a team, the other is almost certain to be chosen with him. Moreover, classmates failed to distinguish between the personality and behaviour of each twin when specifically invited to do so. Koch's (1966) study of twins aged five and six years has similar findings, especially in relation to MZ girls, who were particularly popular. On the other hand the 'closeness' of twins did not appear to interfere with their friendship with other children (self rated) or their involvement with adults, although their teachers described them as slightly less gregarious than the matched singletons in the same class.

A further factor relating to the mother's attitudes is the extent to which she herself is aware of (and responsive to) the differences between the twins. It might be argued, for example, that the mother of identical twins might be more 'vigilant' to any contrasts in personality and behaviour, whereas the mother of DZ twins – who are already sufficiently differentiated by their appearance – might be less sensitive to such differences. Our own study provided some possible confirmation of this paradox. In rating their twins on the Vineland Social Maturity Scale (Doll, 1953), the intra-pair differences were significantly *greater* for the MZ than the DZ pairs, as shown in the intraclass correlation of 0·65 for MZ and 0·96 for DZ twins. This is, of course, directly contrary to what would be predicted on a genetic hypothesis, and tends to suggest, though not conclusively, that mothers of identical twins are more ready than mothers of DZ twins to comment spontaneously on differences in social maturity at least (Mittler, 1969a).

Conclusions

Long before scientists began to study twins, they were objects of curiosity and fascination to their fellow men. Our own attitudes to twins may to some extent carry vestiges of the awe and even veneration in which they were held for thousands of years in most societies. Even today, many people believe that they have special gifts – telepathy may be given as the most obvious example – and there is no doubt that they tend to be very popular in school. On the other hand, we have seen that they are highly vulnerable individuals both biologically and cognitively. Their birth and early development is not without risk, and they tend, as a group, to be somewhat below average in physical and intellectual development.

These factors cannot be lightly set aside by anyone wishing to use twins for research purposes, least of all by psychologists. Twins must be regarded as possessing characteristics which make them an unrepresentative sample of the general population. We have been particularly concerned in this chapter to stress the possible effect of the attitudes of parents and of other people in their environment, though we know next to nothing about ways in which mothers treat twins, and ways in which child rearing practices differ from those found with singleton children. We also know little about their social development. Many writers have discussed the closeness of the twin relationship and their identification with one another, but few carefully conducted studies are available. We have reluctantly to conclude that we know remarkably little about the psychology of twins as individuals.

3 The Twin Method in Psychology

Preoccupation with the origins of human individual differences is by no means new. Plato discusses human differences in terms of an analogy between gold and silver, and in Aristotle's writings there is already a clear awareness of the association between the degree of resemblance and the closeness of the genetic relationship within families. But only in the later decades of the nineteenth century were the origins of such differences systematically explored. Darwin's concept of continuous variation, Mendel's distinction between genotype and phenotype, and the development of appropriate statistical techniques – by Pearson, Fisher and others – all laid essential foundations for later twin studies. Galton (1875) is generally credited with the development of the twin method, though Neel and Schull (1954) quote an earlier paper by Späth (1860) embodying similar ideas.

Reduced to its simplest form, the twin method assumes that any difference within identical pairs must be due to environmental or at least non-genetic causes, whereas differences within fraternal pairs are due to both environmental and genetic factors. The extent to which identical twins resemble each other more than fraternal twins is held to reflect the strength of the genetic contribution to a characteristic.

The basic assumptions involved in twin studies are open to criticism on a number of counts. It is the purpose of this chapter to summarize some of the more important objections to the use of the twin method, and to try to come to some conclusions about its advantages and limitations. Criticisms can be ordered into four groups for purposes of discussion:

1. Methods of determining zygosity.

2. Assumptions relating to genetic similarities and differences.

3. Assumptions concerning equivalence of environmental variables.

4. Differences between twins and singletons.

Zygosity determination

Discussions about the reliability of methods of diagnosing zygosity have swung full circle. Some of the early twin studies which used impressionistic methods of deciding whether twins were identical or fraternal became suspect with the development of more advanced techniques, partticularly blood grouping (serology) and finger and palm print analysis (dermatoglyphics). Although these techniques are now used almost routinely in most twin studies, recent evidence from the World Health Organization studies suggest that their accuracy, which is undoubtedly high, is nevertheless little better than a crude index of similarity, which in the case of adult twins consists merely of asking them whether people had difficulty in telling them apart (Cederlöf, Friberg, Jonson and Kaij, 1961). Methods of diagnosing zygosity are discussed in appendix A; for a fuller treatment of this subject, see Smith and Penrose (1955). In general, it seems reasonable to conclude that the margin of possible error in the allocation of zygosity is now sufficiently small to discount this as a serious criticism of the twin method.

Genetic similarities and differences

More complicated problems arise from a number of genetic assumptions which underlie the use of the twin method.

The most fundamental assumption of the twin method relates to the genetic identity of a monozygotic pair, and to the corollary that any differences between identical pairs must therefore be due to non-genetic factors. It is often further assumed that any differences which are not genetic must be 'environmental'. All attempts by biometricians and psychologists to derive quantifiable heritability indices depend on this basic premise of genetic identity between M Z twins.

This assumption has, however, been questioned by some geneticists. Darlington (1954) for example insists that M Z twins '... must differ on genetic grounds; that is to say, they differ internally at the beginning'. Differences within M Z pairs may originate at the nuclear stage (gene mutations or chromosome errors at mitosis), or in cytoplasmic differences. As examples of the latter, we may consider asymmetries and the mirror image phenomenon which are commonly encountered in identicals (e.g. opposite handedness, hair whorls, etc.).

An important account of 'primary biases' in twin studies has been published by Price (1950). He divides biases into three categories:

1. Natal factors, such as foetal position *in utero*, including crowding, special conditions of implantation, and the nature and order of the delivery.

2. Lateral inversions.

3. The effects of mutual circulation.

These biases can differentially affect the physical and intellectual development of twins, but, as Darlington (1954) points out, their effect is to underestimate the contribution of hereditary factors. He concludes: 'We have to admit that comparisons of one egg and two egg twins do not give us the uncontaminated separation of heredity and environment which Galton and his successors have hoped for' (Darlington, 1963). The embryology of twin development is considerably more complex than was once supposed. In the case of identicals, much depends on the stage of development reached by the zygote before the splitting takes place. When the zygote divides almost immediately, the two halves become implanted in different sites of the uterus, and each develops separately in its own membranes. In the majority of cases, however, (up to 70 per cent according to Scheinfeld, 1968) the egg divides only after some early development has taken place, and the two embryos remain in the same membrane (chorion). An extreme form of late splitting occurs in Siamese twins, who are often, one might think surprisingly, dissimilar in appearance (Gedda, 1961).

Development within a single membrane is thus no guarantee of close similarity, rather the reverse, it seems. Recent studies of the differential rates of intra-uterine development in MZ twins have established that 'foetal crowding' within the same chorion can occur and carries a high risk of one twin obtaining a disproportionately small share of the maternal blood supply. Strong and Corney's (1967) monograph *The Placenta in Twin Pregnancy* summarizes an extensive literature on the 'placental transfusion syndrome' in MZ twins; it appears that, in addition to the circulatory system between each twin and the mother, there is a third circulatory system between the twins themselves; the appearance of any asymmetry in this system later becomes the cause of functional and anatomical alterations in the foetuses. Corney and Aherne (1965) published a study showing gross differences in haemoglobin values in MZ neonates, which they ascribe to twin transfusion in the early months of pregnancy.

Several obstetric and paediatric studies of infant twins indicate that the likelihood of substantial differences in birth weight is greater in MZ pairs than in DZ. The fact that one twin (usually the second born) is exposed to greater intra-uterine hazards is obviously of fundamental significance both to their physical and psychological development in later life. We thus find a paradoxical situation in which twins who are 'genetically identical' may begin their lives under very different developmental conditions, but become more similar as they grow older, unless, of course, one twin sustains injury or damage to such an extent that the genetic 'instructions' for, say, the development of high intelligence, cannot be fulfilled as a result of such damage. By contrast, DZ twins may look quite similar at birth, but the differences between them are likely to become more pronounced as they grow older. These facts have been insufficiently appreciated in studies of the heritability of psychological characteristics such as intelligence which are affected to some extent by certain pre-natal variables more frequently found in MZ than in DZ pairs.

Other genetic assumptions

Any estimate of the relative contribution of genetic and environmental factors to the variance of a test score is of necessity specific to the particular population tested, at that particular time and under those particular environmental conditions. Nothing approaching an 'absolute' answer to any aspect of the 'nature-nurture' question can be expected. Much depends upon the nature of the population, and, as in any other correlation study, upon the variance of the scores within the population as a whole, and within the specific twin population considered as individuals. A highly homogeneous population of twins will, because of the nature of most statistical formulae for correlation, produce a lower association than a more heterogeneous population.

It is clearly of great importance to ensure that any generalizations about the heritability of a characteristic should not be limited to a particular twin population, but should try to make some estimate for the expression of genetic factors in the general population as a whole.

A further difficulty posed by twin studies is the underlying assumption of random mating between parents. Estimates of heritability theoretically assume the need for random mating, although it is well known that husband–wife correlations for intelligence are around 0·5 – in fact very similar to the correlations between sibs, between fraternal twins or between parent and child. Assortative mating would, of course, tend to raise the correlations between offspring, sibs or twins.

Attempts to solve these problems have been made by a number of workers. Jensen (1967, 1969) has proposed somewhat elaborate formulae derived from quantitative genetics which are designed to allow not only for assortative mating, but also for effects due to dominance, to covariance and interaction between heredity and environment, interaction among genes at two or more loci and also errors due to unreliable measures. These formulae are beyond the scope of the present discussion; some methods of deriving heritability estimates are summarized in appendix B; for a fuller discussion of mathematical models see Jinks and Fulker (1970).

It might also be objected that twin children are not really suitable subjects in a genetic study, because the characteristics being investigated are not fully developed. Thus, a number of studies demonstrate increasing parent–child similarities as the child grows up; this has been clearly shown for height (Bayley, 1954) and also for IQ (Skodak and Skeels, 1949); indeed, it is precisely these increasing parent–child similarities that have been advanced in support of arguments for the influence of heredity, especially when such similarities can be demonstrated in children who have been separated from their true parents since birth.

On the other hand, studies of adult twins come up against intractable sampling problems, since representative adult twins are hard to find and even harder to recruit. Volunteer bias is marked when appeals are made through television, as has happened in a number of recent studies (Shields, 1962; Huntley, 1966).

Twin studies that have used children as subjects can also be criticized for paying insufficient attention to age. Many studies use children of all ages, thereby confounding the genetic with the developmental variables, since the characteristic under investigation is likely to be at different stages of maturity across the sample. This disadvantage is not removed by administering a test such as the Wechsler or Terman–Merrill Intelligence Scales which can be given over a wide age range, since not only does the item content vary with age, but the evidence of factorial studies suggests that the test is measuring different skills at different ages.

One other genetic problem needs to be mentioned, relating to the degree of expected similarity of fraternal twins. Although it is true that fraternal twins have 50 per cent of their genes in common, this statement merely describes an average; actual similarities clearly vary widely around this average, depending on how the genes are 'shuffled out'. There are some fraternal pairs who resemble each other quite closely, whereas others may look so different that they are not even suspected of being siblings. Geneticists express this point by stressing that 'the hereditary component in the fraternal twin differences consists not only of an additive component but includes also a genic component which is the effect of that combination of genes which is unique for each individual, and which is not transmitted to the individual's offspring' (Vandenberg, 1968a, p. 229). However, this problem can be partially overcome by collecting data on other relatives, particularly other siblings and parents; Cattell's (1965a) Multiple Abstract Variance Analysis provides the relevant model for this kind of study.

Environmental sources of within-pair differences

Possible differences between MZ twins are not, of course, limited to the pre-natal period. It has been suggested that it is precisely their genetic and physical similarity which may in time tend to emphasize and even exaggerate any differences between them. As they become older each twin is more likely, on this argument, to be impelled to seek his own individuality by accentuating those characteristics which differentiate him from his co-twin. This may be relatively easier in the non-cognitive sphere; the evidence for genetic factors in personality, though increasingly impressive, is not as strong as for cognitive skills. Many clinical studies, for example, report that one twin is dominant over the other, or more commonly acts as a spokesman, and there are examples of role playing in which twins appear to 'change personalities', perhaps partly as a game (Zazzo, 1960). Over half the mothers in our study had no difficulty in deciding which twin was dominant.

The classical twin study method is open to criticism for confusing the genuinely greater physical and genetic similarity of MZ twins with the greater environmental similarity to which they might be exposed as a result of parents, siblings and peers treating them in the same way. Any environmentally created similarities, would, of course, tend to increase the similarities between identical twins, and lend spurious support to a genetic interpretation of the data.

This possibility was checked by Scarr (1966, 1969) as part of a wider twin study. She studied mothers of twin girls who were correct or incorrect in their estimates of the zygosity of their twins by asking them to complete a check list of personality ratings of their children, and also of their own child-rearing practices. Her thesis was as follows: 'If MZ pairs, thought to be DZ, were rated like other MZ pairs, the mothers were probably not creating additional similarities by their treatment of the children. But if MZ pairs, thought to be DZ, were rated like other DZ pairs, then the mothers were responding to their beliefs about the twins and probably biasing the results. Similar predictions apply to DZ twins whose mothers believed them to be MZ twins' (1966, p. 668). There were, in fact, no significant differences between correctly and incorrectly identified pairs on any of her measures, thus confirming her first proposition that the incorrectly identified pairs were rated and treated like other pairs of their actual zygosity. Scarr concluded that 'the mothers tended to respond to the genetic similarities and differences of their twins, regardless of whether they believed the twins should or should not resemble each other'.

Nevertheless, the numbers in her study were very small, and it is probably reasonable to conclude that there is little empirical justification for the basic assumption of the twin method to the effect that the environmental contribution to the within-pair variance of a characteristic is the same for identical and fraternal twins. As Vandenberg (1966) points out, this assumption is an over-simplification, since heredity and environment interact, but 'in twin studies the variance due to this interaction is usually grouped with the variance due to heredity'.

Another way of approaching the same problem is to study differences rather than similarities within pairs, and also to examine the stability of such differences over a period of time. A recent study by Vandenberg and his associates (Brown, Stafford and Vandenberg, 1967) was specifically concerned with discordance between M Z twins, and showed that the twin rated lower on behavioural characteristics, such as feeding and sleeping problems, tempers, crying etc., showed consistent patterns in his early history – e.g. in birth weight and birth sequence.

Only a longitudinal study with relatively large numbers of subjects can provide the relevant information, but virtually no published reports of longitudinal studies are available for twins, though several are in progress (e.g. Witherspoon, 1965; Vandenberg, 1968a). It seems likely, however, that family variables will need to be studied in some detail, and with methods somewhat more refined than in the past, in order to assess, for example, whether and in what respects parents with large families treat their twins differently from those with small families; the extent to which parents perceive (or report) differences between their twins, treat them alike in respect of presents, etc., and how far they dress them alike. Differences in parental behaviour in these respects can usefully be examined in relation to social class, size of family and other social factors.

Longitudinal studies would provide even more useful information on the psychological development of twins than they have already done for normal children; they could include data on rates of development of twins in general and of the various subgroups of different zygosity and sex. They would also throw light on the relationship between the year to year development of specific cognitive skills and environmental variables such as parental language, socio-economic factors, family size, etc. Furthermore, an inspection of extreme groups could be usefully carried out – for example, twins showing the fastest and slowest rates of development could be examined individually with a view to isolating factors in the child or in his environment which might be associated with his particular developmental profile. Finally, within-pair differences could be analysed in the same detail. Studies of separated twins are also relevant in any consideration of environmental bias. These are more fully reviewed in later chapters, but we may anticipate here the conclusion that they have not provided strong evidence of such bias. On the contrary, many of them have tended to suggest that correlations for separated identical twins on a number of characteristics are only slightly lower, and sometimes insignificantly different, from correlations obtained for identical twins brought up together (Shields, 1962; Wilde, 1964; Vandenberg and Johnson, 1968).

Although only a small number of separated twins have been studied, the absence of marked effects of separation is more clearly seen in personality than in intelligence tests. This situation has led Eysenck (1967) to conclude that the higher correlations for separated twins are a reflection of the development of the individual's 'true' personality, unaffected by the presence of the co-twin. It is only when twins are brought up together, on this argument, that the effect of each twin on the other, and the common effect of the environment on each twin, may well combine to hamper the development of genetically determined aspects of personality. More studies are needed to justify such an interpretation, but it does seem likely that insufficient weight has been given to the effects on the development of personality of factors specific to 'the twin situation'. Furthermore, it may also be misleading to assume, as most twin studies have always done, that 'the environment of MZ twins living together is the same'.

Twin–singleton differences

Enough evidence has already been provided in chapter 2 to indicate that twins are in certain respects not a representative sample of the general population. Not only are they subject to very different biological and developmental hazards from the moment of conception, but as a group, they show consistent, if slight, inferiority in respect of their intellectual functioning and educational skills throughout the whole of their childhood. Any generalizations relating to the general population which are based exclusively on the study of twins are therefore founded in a logical difficulty which does not so far appear to have been met. Although the logic of the twin method assumes the necessity for a 'substantial equivalence of twins and the general population with respect to the trait studied' (Fuller and Thompson, 1960, p. 110), this criterion is usually ignored by psychologists in making heritability estimates. The logical problem is straightforward: how far is it permissible to draw inferences about the heritability of a continuously graded characteristic such as 'intelligence' in the general population from a study of twins, who, as individuals, show a different distribution of scores and lower mean values?

Bias due to sampling artefacts in the twin population can be overcome. It is important to ensure that a twin sample being used to examine the influence of heredity on intelligence test scores should at least be normally distributed and show mean scores at or near IQ 100, with a SD of fifteen. Fully representative samples of twins might well fall below this level; in practice, volunteer bias may spuriously raise the mean IQ of the sample.

Conclusions

In this chapter we have tried to outline some of the basic assumptions on which twin studies have been founded, together with their advantages and limitations. For example, it is not certain that identical twins are necessarily genetically identical; differences may be present from the moment of conception which can affect differentially both physical and psychological development. In fact, their pre-natal and early post-natal development may follow a divergent course at this early stage, only to converge later towards greater similarity. Fraternal twins, on the other hand, may be more similar as infants than as children or adults. Identical twins are more vulnerable than fraternals to complications of pregnancy and delivery, and hence to later neurological and psychological difficulties. The use of the twin method involves a number of other assumptions which call for critical scrutiny. Even the most carefully conducted twin study can only yield findings which apply to a particular population studied at a given age and under given environmental circumstances. The same results need not necessarily be expected from a different twin population, especially if it is not developmentally comparable. A related problem concerns the legitimacy of deriving conclusions about the heritability of a characteristic in the general population from a study of twins, who as individuals are not representative of that population.

Environmental sources of bias have also been insufficiently studied. We cannot yet be sure that parental attitudes and treatment do not complicate the issue by emphasizing existing similarities or creating new ones. We know very little of the 'natural history' of the twin situation, and how parents perceive the similarities and differences within a twin pair. The few studies which look at this question do not suggest that a serious source of bias arises in parental attitudes, but more investigation is needed. It seems likely that future research will be more concerned with twin differences rather than similarities, and with attempts to relate possible consistencies in behaviour with aspects of the twin relationship itself, and also with the constellations of behaviour in the families of twins.

Despite the various sources of bias and error inherent in the twin method, there has nevertheless proved to be a sufficient consistency in the findings of many researchers working with differing populations and a variety of techniques to justify the continued use of twins as unique sources of evidence in our attempts to understand at least some of the factors contributing to the development of individuality.

Two other considerations are relevant. In the first place, we can compare the results of twin studies with other approaches to the study of the heredity–environment problem, especially pedigree and family studies involving multivariate methods of analysis. Secondly, we can study characteristics in which sources of bias are under greater control. It is unlikely, for example, that environmental factors of the kind discussed above would appreciably influence the development of characteristics such as height and weight or patterns of psychophysiological response. For this reason, we shall begin our review of twin research by an examination of some of these biological aspects of development. We shall then be in a better position to assess possible sources of error in the use of the twin method applied to the study of intelligence and personality.

Part Two Findings

4 Biological Factors

In their preoccupation with intellect, psychologists have tended to neglect biological aspects of behaviour. This neglect has been particularly unfortunate in twin studies, since many biological characteristics lend themselves to much more precise and reliable measurement than the traditional measures of intelligence and personality. Moreover, interactions between heredity and environment which complicate the interpretation of most psychological investigations are not quite so much in evidence for height, weight, physiological and autonomic functioning, and sensory and motor processes.

It is convenient to think of a continuum at one end of which are clustered characteristics in which the environmental component is either absent or minimal – eye colour and finger ridge count are obvious examples – and at the other end of which one finds behaviours in which the genetic component plays a minimal part, or which are too complex for the question even to be posed in the present state of knowledge. Intermediate between these extremes we can find variables such as height, which while mainly genetic in origin, are nevertheless open to environmental influences, while others, such as aspects of personality, temperament or character are probably more strongly affected by environmental factors, even though a genetic factor can be shown to be relevant to at least some aspects of personality as well.

Although psychologists have, not surprisingly, devoted most of their energies to the investigation of twins' cognitive skills, it is worth remembering that 'intelligence' and cognitive skills are built on biological foundations. To function intellectually, we need an intact and effective central nervous system, not merely anatomically, but also physiologically and biochemically, since the system has to be able to accept, code and classify complex sensory information, and to react appropriately. We no longer make sharp distinctions between sensation and perception, or between perception and intelligence, but regard human behaviour as a hierarchy of interacting activities and processes. Thus, intelligence, even as measured by classical intelligence tests, cannot be satisfactorily separated from more basic biological processes.

In this chapter, we shall discuss a selection of twin studies that have examined anthropometric measures such as height and weight; physiological data, including studies of EEG, autonomic functioning, galvanic skin response and sedation threshold; sensory and perceptual processes and motor skills. Some co-twin control studies will also be reviewed.

Anthropometric studies

The study of anthropometric measures may, as Vandenberg (1966) points out, act both as a model and as a benchmark for work in human behaviour genetics:

as a model to the extent that traits such as height and shoulder width are (a) quantitative traits, (b) probably under the control of many genes, and (c) somewhat modified by environmental conditions; as a benchmark because results so far have shown much higher values for Holzinger's h^2 (or for the F-ratio for anthropometric variables) than for behavioural measures (p. 337).

In an earlier review, he summarized six studies showing a broad measure of agreement (Vandenberg, 1962); similarly, Burt (1966) compared his own results with those of Newman, Freeman and Holzinger (1937), while Huntley (1966) in a large scale study compared 320 twin pairs with their own parents and siblings. Their findings, and those of our own study of a group of four-year-old twins (Mittler 1969a), for height and weight only, are shown in Table 1.

Examination of this table can leave little doubt that

Table 1

Intraclass Correlation and Heritability (Holziger's H and Falconer's h^2) for Height and Weight of MZ Pairs Brought Up Together (MZ_t), Brought Up Apart (MZ_a) and DZ Pairs.

	Height					Weight				
	MZ_t	MZ_a	DZ	H	h^2	MZ_t	MZ_a	DZ	H	h^2
Newman, Freeman and Holzinger, 1937	0·93	0·97	0·64	0·38	0·58	0·92	0·89	0·63	0·38	0·58
Shields, 1962	0·96	0·82	0·44	0·93	1·04	0·80	0·87	0·56	0·54	0·48
Burt, 1966 (several studies)	0·96	0·94	0·47	0·92	0·98	0·93	0·88	0·59	0·55	0·68
Huntley, 1966	0·90		0·58	0·76	0·64					
Mittler, 1969a	0·91		0·48	0·82	0·86	0·89		0·51	0·77	0·76

identical twins, whether separated or not, are highly correlated in respect of height, when compared to fraternals,
and that resemblances, though still strong, are slightly less
marked for weight.

These findings suggest that genetic factors account for a
substantial part of the variance of height measurements.
The Falconer h^2 calculations are obviously only approxi-
mations, but they do indicate that between 60 and 80 per
cent of the variance is genetic in origin. Comparisons with
our own study indicate that degrees of resemblances are
similar whether twins are homogeneous for age (i.e. all
exactly four years old, and therefore still partly grown) or
whether, as in the other studies, they are at different ages
and stages of physical development.

It will be recalled that twins fall slightly but significantly
below population norms during childhood and at least up to
eighteen years (Husén, 1959). Physical development is ideally
considered from a longitudinal point of view, and involves
the fitting of 'growth curves' to determine the pattern of
growth increments in different populations – e.g. M Z and
D Z twins, siblings, unrelated children, etc. Most investigators have had to convert measures of height and weight
to standard scores when dealing with a wide age range.
Radiological studies of bone development are now becoming more widely used, since these can yield a 'bone age',
which is considered to be one of the most reliable criteria
of physiological maturity (Garn, 1966). Dental, facial and
body-build indices have also been reported. Vandenberg
(1962) concluded that there was so much agreement between
many studies that further work was not justified, unless
multivariate methods of analysis were employed. Further
evidence of hereditary influences on height is provided by
studies of Japanese immigrants to Hawaii and the USA
which show surprisingly small, though significant, differences
with relatives remaining in Japan (Kaplan, 1954, cited by
Vandenberg, 1966).

Autonomic variables

One of the earliest physiological researches was that of Jost and Sontag (1944) who worked with a very small and heterogeneous sample of twins. MZ twins showed greater similarity than siblings on an overall index of 'autonomic stability' made up of breathing rate, blood pressure, perspiration and pulse rate. A more recent study from the Pavlov Institute in Leningrad has shown high concordance in MZ twins for changes of blood pressure and skin temperature following systematic exposure to hot or cold stimuli, and also for blood pressure changes following auditory and visual stimulation (Kryshova *et al*, 1963). Similar results were reported by Vandenberg, Clark and Samuels (1965) in reactions to mild stress by changes in heartbeat frequency and respiration rate, but they failed to establish regular patterns of galvanic skin response. Other studies of physiological interest concern the onset of menarche showing a mean difference of 2·8 months for MZ and 12·0 for DZ twin girls (Petri, 1934). Interestingly enough, mothers and daughters showed no closer relationship in this respect than unrelated women. At the other end of the age scale, it seems that the age of senescence and death is more similar for MZ than for DZ twins (Jarvik, Kallmann and Klaber, 1957).

Preliminary studies of autonomic function have been reported by a team of Finnish investigators (Lehtovaara, Saarinen and Jarvinen, 1965). They measured the effect of exposing pictures of varying emotive content on measures of the galvanic skin response (GSR) and showed that some measures showed far higher heritability than others: for example, total frequency and form of GSR seemed to be much more influenced by hereditary factors than the areas of the reaction curve. Claridge and his associates at the University of Glasgow have also reported preliminary findings suggestive of higher MZ than DZ correlations for the orienting response and spontaneous fluctuations of skin potential, and for initial heart rate levels (Hume, 1969);

Claridge (in press) found significantly higher M Z than D Z
correlations on a measure of sedation threshold – i.e. the
amount of a sedative drug (sodium amytal) injected before
a subject begins to fail on a simple test requiring him to
double numbers; previous work by Shagass had suggested
that sedation threshold varied according to ratings on di-
mensions of obsessionality-hysteria. Nine out of eleven M Z
pairs had differences of one milligram per kilo of body
weight (an extremely small difference), whereas eight of ten
D Z pairs differed by more than this amount. Nevertheless,
examination of individual pairs revealed two M Z pairs with
very large differences, possibly due in one case to differences
in the intra-uterine environment and a very difficult birth.

Mention should be made of a careful study of hormonal
steroid patterns, which have also been tenuously related
to personality: by using discriminant function analysis,
Fox *et al.* (1965, 1970), showed that M Z twins could be distinguished from non-twins by their steroid excretion
patterns, particularly seventeen ketosteroids and seventeen
hydroxicorticosteroids.

It might have been expected that studies of autonomic
functioning in newborn or infant twins would have been
published, but no advantage has yet been taken of the refinements of measuring and recording techniques which are
seen in the work of investigators such as Lipsitt (1966) or
Lipton and his associates (1966). It would be interesting, for
example, to test Vandenberg's speculation that subjects who
respond to stress primarily with heart rate changes may have
similar reactions at later ages, and be more vulnerable to
coronary disease, whereas infants who respond in terms of
GSR changes may be more prone to allergic and derma-
tological disorders.

Electro-cortical activity

A considerable number of studies of electroencephalo-
graphic (EEG) activity have been reported, most of them
showing striking similarity of EEG patterns in identical

twins (Fuller and Thompson, 1960). Most of the earlier work depended on visual inspection of EEG records rather than on the kind of precise quantitative analysis which is now possible as a result of developments in the use of on-line methods of computer analysis (Lennox, Gibbs and Gibbs, 1954; Juel-Nielsen and Harvald, 1958). Nevertheless EEG workers were agreed that the records showed striking similarities, and could often be physically superimposed on one another.

The development of computer analysis, and particularly of averaging techniques, has opened up new possibilities for the study of genetic aspects of central nervous system functioning. In a study carried out in Birmingham, Clarke and Harding (1969) compared ten normal M Z with ten like-sex DZ pairs aged eight years. Although the records of the M Z pairs were not found to be more similar than those of DZ pairs on visual inspection only, computer frequency analysis of the harmonic means indicated significant differences for the non-dominant, but not for the dominant hemisphere. This finding should be related to studies which suggest that genetic factors may play a more important role in the development of visuo-spatial than of verbal abilities (see chapter 5).

Even more precise methods of EEG quantification can be expected from work on 'evoked cortical potentials'. This technique permits analysis of the exact constituents of the cortical response to a specific signal, such as flashes of light or pure tones. Furthermore, the various components of the response can be separately analysed.

Dustman and Beck (1965) have reported a comparison of visually evoked potential to 100 light flashes in twelve pairs of M Z and eleven pairs of DZ twins, and in a control group of twelve pairs of unrelated children matched for age. They analysed the wave components for the first 250 milliseconds and the first 400 milliseconds, and also compared central with occipital recordings. Results are summarized in Table 2.

Further analyses of variance indicated that the major

Table 2

Correlations of Evoked Responses from MZ, DZ and Unrelated Children Matched for Age

Group	Site of recording	Mean correlations 0–250 ms	0–400 ms
MZ	Occipital	0·82	0·81
	Central	0·74	0·69
DZ	Occipital	0·58	0·54
	Central	0·48	0·41
Unrelated children	Occipital	0·61	0·56
	Central	0·53	0·49

Source: Dustman and Beck (1965)

differences were between groups, and that differences were also more significant for the first components (i.e. the first 250 ms) than for later components (the first 400 ms). They also reported individual analyses in which an identical twin's evoked response was more like that of his twin sib than like another of his own evoked responses recorded between one and six months later. Comparison of correlations for identical (0·82) and fraternal (0·58) twins (occipital recording) shows obvious similarities with intelligence and other psychometric data, and suggests that some 57 per cent of the variance is genetic (Holzinger's *H*). On the other hand, it must be noted that fraternal twins were no different from unrelated pairs of the same age who were artificially 'twinned' for the purposes of the experiment.

Sensory and perceptual functions

Studies of sensory and perceptual processes have been largely concerned with estimating concordance rates for specific abnormalities and pathological sensory conditions, particularly of the eye. Genetic abnormalities of vision have been described for over 100 years, while Pickford (1951) has described individual differences in colour vision. Detailed perceptual tests have been carried out for size of after-image and eidetic imagery (Smith, 1949), the Muller–Leyer illusion, the autokinetic phenomenon and critical flicker fusion (Eysenck and Prell, 1951). A review of earlier studies may be found in Fuller and Thompson (1960). The results of some of these studies are summarized in Table 3.

Table 3

Intraclass Correlations and Heritabilities
(Holzinger's H and Falconer's h^2) on Perceptual Tasks

	MZ	DZ	H	h^2
Size of after-image	0·71	0·08	0·68	1·26
(four tests) (Smith, 1949)	0·68	0·00	0·68	1·36
	0·98	0·22	0·97	1·52
	0·75	0·23	0·67	1·04
Eidetic imagery	0·50	0·10	0·44	0·80
(three measures) (Smith,	0·66	0·15	0·60	1·02
1949)	0·67	0·05	0·65	1·24
Muller–Leyer illusion,	0·53	0·39	0·22	0·28
four conditions of	0·55	0·05	0·52	1·00
presentation (Smith, 1953)	0·51	0·37	0·22	0·28
	0·57	0·28	0·40	0·58
Critical flicker fusion	0·71	0·21	0·63	1·00
(Eysenck and Prell, 1951)				
Autokinetic phenomenon	0·72	0·21	0·64	1·02
(Eysenck and Prell, 1951)				

It will be seen that the tests generally reflect high heritability, but that values are not necessarily consistent even within four different presentations of a single type of task. Thus, reliability of the measures must affect heritability estimates. Heritability ratios are themselves subject to error; for example, Falconer's h^2 gives absurdly high values for some of the measures, since it is impossible for more than 100 per cent of the variance to be accounted for by genetic factors. For this reason, both Holzinger's H and Falconer's h^2 have been calculated for purposes of comparison.

Handedness

Since motor skills are perhaps more directly under the control of the nervous system, students of behaviour genetics have been particularly interested in comparing MZ and DZ twins on a variety of motor functions; these tests also have the advantage of being more convenient to administer and many of them have good reliability. It appears that the genetic component is more strongly in evidence when the right (or dominant) hand is being tested. Interestingly enough, handwriting is an exception to the rule of higher MZ than DZ correlations; several studies have shown as big differences in handwriting for identical as for fraternal twins and siblings (Husén, 1959). It has been suggested that handwriting represents too fine a degree of psychomotor coordination to be subject to genetic control to the same extent as less highly developed skills (Newman, Freeman and Holzinger, 1937).

This problem is complicated by reports of a higher frequency of left handedness in twins: earlier studies (summarized by Rife, 1940) suggested that between 10 and 12 per cent of twins were sinistrals, while Zazzo (1960) in a later summary of ten studies involving over 2300 pairs, showed that the percentage of left-handed twins was 16·1 for MZ and 12·9 for DZ twins. These findings were not confirmed by Husén (1959) who reported on the basis of an inquiry involving nearly 3000 twin and 4500 singleborn conscripts that the proportion was 6 per cent in both groups, and that the frequency of left handedness was the same for MZ and DZ twins. Further complexities are introduced by the fact that an unknown proportion of twins show opposite handedness patterns. Husén's estimate (1959) is 12 per cent for both MZ and DZ pairs, whereas Zazzo's is almost twice as high (MZ 24·4 per cent, DZ 22·1 per cent). In view of the association in singleton children between left handedness and speech and language delays (Ingram, 1965, Lenneberg, 1967) it might have been expected that left-handed twins would show lower scores on a standardized test of language abilities, but this was not found to be the case in our own study comparing left- and right-handed twins on the Illinois Test of Psycholinguistic Abilities (Mittler, 1970c).

We must conclude that both the facts and the significance of the facts about handedness and asymmetries are still in dispute. A fairly convincing hypothesis to account for the finding that left handedness is more common in identical than in fraternal twins has been put forward by Newman, Freeman and Holzinger (1937), who pointed out that one twin is derived from a partially differentiated left, and the other from a partially differentiated right half of a single embryo. But the problem is to account for the higher incidence of left handedness in fraternal twins, who develop from two independent zygotes.

Motor skills

Perhaps the fullest study of motor skills was carried out by McNemar (1933) on nine pairs of junior age twins. An unusual variation on the conventional approach in his study was the examination of the effects of practice on within-pair differences. The results of three tests of motor skills are summarized in Table 4.

It is apparent that practice has little or no effect on the scores of MZ pairs, but that DZ pairs tend to show reduced differences on at least two of the three tests. Similar results were reported by Brody (1937). Although these findings are no more than suggestive, they support the important point made by Smith (1949), following his studies of changes in the Muller–Leyer illusion as a result of repeated practice: 'It seems advisable not to confine heredity–psychological

Table 4

Intraclass Correlations and Heritabilities (Holzinger's
H and Falconer's h^2 before and after Practice on a Series
of Motor Tasks

		MZ (N = 45)	DZ (N = 46)	H	h^2
Koerth Pursuit	Initial	0·88	0·44	0·78	0·88
Rotor	Final	0·87	0·60	0·67	0·54
Spool packing	Initial	0·56	0·38	0·29	0·36
	Final	0·54	0·55	0·00	0·02
Card sorting	Initial	0·75	0·56	0·43	0·38
	Final	0·71	0·49	0·43	0·44

Source: McNemar (1933)

investigations to traditional performance scores. . . . The
concept of heredity in psychology must be looked upon as
basically developmental.' In this context, development may
cover a short experimental session, or the whole life span of
the twin subjects. It seems important to check the suggestion
in McNemar's data that MZ within pair differences are
unaffected by practice, whereas DZ pairs tend to become
more similar in performance of at least some tasks. This
would result in reduced heritabilities for the final as compared to the initial test.

Co-twin control studies

No mention has been made so far of the method of co-twin
control as a means of throwing light on the relative contribution of genetic and non-genetic factors on development.
Several ambitious studies using this technique were published in the 1930s, most of them concerned with aspects of
motor skill, but occasionally with language (Strayer, 1930;
Luria and Yudovitch, 1959).

In essence, the method consists of giving training in a skill to only one identical twin, while using the other as a control. It was hoped by comparing both twins after training only one that it would be possible to see whether changes of behaviour could be attributed to maturation or to learning. Findings have not in general been particularly impressive or conclusive, but some of the better known studies will now be briefly summarized.

The best known studies were those of Gesell and Thompson (1929, 1941) and Hilgard (1933) using the same pair of twin girls. In the Gesell study, Twin T was given a period of six weeks' intensive training in stair climbing and in manipulating cubes at the age of forty-two weeks. After T had completed her training, C was given a two week training period. Although T was still climbing better than C several weeks later, C needed less practice to reach the same level of proficiency. It was also noted that C's attitude was more anxious and dependent.

Hilgard's experiment (1933) with the same pair was somewhat better designed, and took the form of an initial test, eight weeks training of T, retest, eight weeks training of C, followed by three more retests. A variety of tasks was chosen for training, including tests of digit and object retention, paper-cutting, board-walking and ring-tossing. The results showed that the girls were at almost the same levels both at the beginning and end of the study. Early training produced a slower *rate* of learning than later training, but made no difference to the *level* finally attained. Various interpretations have been given to this study; perhaps maturation emerges as more important than training, but both are clearly relevant.

The best documented co-twin study is undoubtedly in McGraw's book (1935) *Growth: A Study of Johnny and Jimmy*, but unfortunately it was later established that they were not after all identical. McGraw distinguished between 'phylogenetic' activities, such as movement and reaching, and 'ontogenetic' activities such as climbing, jumping, and object attainment tasks similar to those given to Kohler's apes (1925). The trained twin made much greater progress in the ontogenetic than in phylogenetic activities. Attitude remained more positive in the trained twin for many months.

A Russian study (Mirenva, 1935, cited by Newman, Freeman and Holzinger, 1937) used a different approach, by not providing training to the control at any stage. The trained twin was not only superior to his control on the tasks on which he was trained, but there appeared to be some generalization to motor proficiency and even to IQ.

Since these early studies, very few research workers have used the co-twin control method. Objections can be levelled against it on a number of counts. In the first place, everything depends on the timing of the experiment. The experimenter has to use his judgement to decide whether T is 'ready' to benefit from training, since no amount of training will be of any use if it is unduly premature. Similarly, if he waits too long, the skill will appear 'naturally' just as the training is beginning, thereby confounding learning and maturation. Secondly, care has to be taken to ensure that both children are at exactly the same stage of development before training is given to one. Even identical twins may show differences in motor skills, and it is not easy to ensure that measurements of motor skills are reliable at such an early age. Thirdly, it is necessary to produce convincing evidence that the untrained twin is really deprived of all relevant training experiences. This may involve a twenty-four hour vigil to ensure that T is not surreptitiously instructing C, or that C is not impelled by jealousy or curiosity to imitate or at least observe his twin's activities. Finally, it must be observed that the results of the co-twin studies are by no means conclusive one way or the other.

In general, however, co-twin studies have usually been interpreted as giving support to a 'maturational' viewpoint, and have been regarded as evidence supplementary to similar studies by Dennis (1941) and others purporting to show that Hopi Indian children who are strapped in cradle boards for the first few months walk at the same time as those who are allowed more freedom to sit or crawl. Nevertheless, there is scope for refinement of the co-twin control method, particularly if care is taken to choose an appropriate and not altogether obvious skill.

In case an ambitious parent is tempted to embark on a co-twin project, it should be emphasized that such studies would benefit from a truly longitudinal approach, which might include the differential training of different skills in each twin, thus ensuring that both received the same amount of attention, but different training content. More rigorous statistical evaluation would also be welcome, possibly involving a repeated measures design.

Conclusions

Although psychologists have paid far less attention to biological than to cognitive variables, there is a considerable body of evidence to suggest a substantial genetic factor in at least some measures of sensory and motor behaviour. Evidence is derived both from correlational and co-twin control studies.

Such findings are important for at least two reasons. In the first place, it is clear that no sharp distinction can be drawn between biological variables involving sensory, perceptual, motor or autonomic functions on the one hand, and 'intelligence' and other cognitive skills on the other. Secondly, many of the classical objections levelled against the study of intelligence or personality do not apply with anything like the same force or relevance to basic physiological processes. Height and other anthropometric data can not only be measured with greater precision than intelligence, but are less affected by environmental biases springing from the dynamics of the twin relationship, differential treatment of one twin by parents and similar factors. The fact that identical twins are more similar than fraternals in respect of height, electrical activity of the brain, autonomic functioning and basic sensory processes can hardly be attributed to the fact that they are treated in a more uniform way by their parents and by others in their environment, nor can their close relationship to each other be invoked as an explanation. Although such objections can be made in respect of higher mental processes, results of twin studies of intelligence are not markedly different from those of physiological processes, as we shall show in the following chapter.

5 Cognitive Processes

Although no one in possession of the evidence could seriously dispute that genetic factors affect the development of intelligence, there is still much room for argument about the nature and quality of the influence. Unfortunately, the controversies surrounding this question have engendered more heat than light, partly because sharp dichotomies have been created between 'heredity' and 'environment' despite the complex interaction between them.

Although many studies suggest that genetic sources of variance cannot be ignored in accounting for individual differences both within and between populations, current methods of estimating the influence of hereditary sources of variance cannot justify sweeping generalizations about the heritability of a characteristic in the population as a whole; they are limited to one estimate based on one particular sample living in one environment at a particular time. Studies conducted under different environmental conditions, using different samples or a variety of populations could conceivably reach conclusions rather different from those reported up to now.

With these reservations in mind, we can now consider a number of attempts to estimate the contribution of genetic sources of variance to intelligence test scores. These studies have on the whole yielded remarkably consistent findings. Nevertheless, comprehensive examination of these questions calls not merely for more and better twin studies, but for investigations sampling other family relationships – siblings reared apart and together, parent–child, cousins, etc. Such studies can now be launched with more technical sophistication, but their interpretation depends on specialized knowledge of advanced quantitative genetics; Cattell (1965a), for example, advocates the use of multivariate methods of analysis involving various degrees of kinship.

The most extensive summary of kinship similarities in intelligence tests is that of Erlenmeyer-Kimling and Jarvik (1963). This review was based on fifty-two independent investigations from eight countries and four continents, and

Table 5

Correlation Coefficients for 'Intelligence' Test Scores from Fifty-two Studies

Relationship		*Correlations*		
		Median	*Approximate range*	*Number of groups*
Unrelated persons	Reared apart	−0·01	−0·03 – 0·30	4
	Reared together	0·23	0·15 – 0·32	5
Fosterparent–child		0·20	0·18 – 0·38	3
Parent–child		0·50	0·23 – 0·80	12
Siblings	Reared apart	0·40	0·35 – 0·46	2
	Reared together	0·49	0·32 – 0·78	35
Twins				
DZ	Opposite sex	0·53	0·40 – 0·65	9
	Like sex	0·53	0·45 – 0·88	11
MZ	Reared apart	0·75	0·63 – 0·85	4
	Reared together	0·87	0·76 – 0·95	14

Source: Erlenmeyer-Kimling and Jarvik (1963)

included over 30,000 correlational pairings. Since the publication of their review, further reports have appeared – particularly those of Burt (1966), Huntley (1966) and Vandenberg (1965, 1966, 1968a); these confirm the trend of the evidence published by Erlenmeyer-Kimling and Jarvik, whose findings are summarized in Table 5.

A general upward trend of correlations is evident in these

results, but the range obtained for each type of relationship is considerable. This range is likely to be due to the wide range of tests, to the age range of the subjects, and to substantial differences in experimental design. It can be argued, however, that these studies, taken as a group, and accepting their heterogeneous design and execution, constitute a formidable case for the role of hereditary factors in 'intelligence'. Few would now dispute such an interpretation, though there remains much room for doubt about the mechanisms and processes involved. Nevertheless, the median values approximate remarkably closely to the theoretical values that would be expected on a genetic hypothesis, with correlations increasing regularly with increasing degrees of kinship.

Twins reared apart

Studies of separated twins could be of fundamental interest, but there are serious practical difficulties not only in finding separated twins but also in ensuring that they are sufficiently representative of non-separated twins and of the general population. The assumption behind such studies is basically simple: since identical twins share the same genes, any differences between them should be due to environmental factors; the effect of such environmental differences can therefore be conveniently studied in twins brought up in different homes. The practical difficulties and problems of interpretation may be illustrated by considering the main studies.

The earliest and best known investigation is that of Newman and his associates (Newman, Freeman and Holzinger, 1937) who reported in detail on nineteen pairs of separated M Z twins, as well as fifty M Z and fifty D Z pairs brought up together. A large battery of tests was administered, including the Stanford–Binet and Otis tests, together with tests of educational attainment and four tests of personality and temperament (see chapter 6). Detailed biographical and case histories are also included: indeed, these provide a more vivid illustration of the complexities of disentangling nature-nurture interactions than the statistical treatment of test results of this or any other twin investigation. Unfortunately, biographical evidence is not usually considered of sufficient scientific standing, though Newman's examples generally provide rich confirmation of the psychometric evidence. The latter is briefly summarized in Table 6 for nine of the physical and mental measures on which data were available for all types of twin.

Table 6

Correlations for Physical and Mental Tests for MZ Twins Brought Up Together and Apart, and for DZ Twins

	MZ_t ($N = 50$)	MZ_a ($N = 19$)	DZ_t
Standing height	0·981	0·969	0·934
Sitting height	0·965	0·960	0·901
Weight	0·973	0·886	0·900
Head length	0·910	0·917	0·691
Head width	0·908	0·880	0·654
Binet mental age	0·922	0·637	0·831
Binet IQ	0·910	0·670	0·640
Otis IQ	0·922	0·727	0·621
Stanford Achievement	0·955	0·507	0·883

Source: Newman, Freeman and Holzinger (1937)

The table indicates that correlations for physical characteristics are very similar whether MZ twins are brought up together or apart (except for weight); those for intelligence (Binet and Otis IQ) are somewhat affected by separation, whereas those for educational attainment show the strongest influence of environment. The Binet and Otis IQs (though not the Binet Mental Age) for separated MZ pairs show higher correlations for separated identical pairs than for fraternal pairs brought up together. However, the differences are small, and not statistically significant (partly due to the small sample). All that can be concluded is that different environments certainly have some effect on the development of intelligence, but that the extent of the influence varies both with the type of test used and with the extent of the environmental differences. Newman concluded that 'the role of heredity and environment in producing twin differences is a function of the type of environment. Thus, for twins reared together, most of the difference between members of a pair may be due to the nature factor, whereas for twins reared under *strikingly* different environments, the nurture factors will have relatively greater influence' (Newman, Freeman and Holzinger, 1937, p. 349) [added italics].

This conclusion, expressed in terms of 'threshold variables' is supported by the case histories. Thus, twins brought up in 'strikingly different' environments include the celebrated Helen and Gladys, who showed an IQ difference of twenty-four points at the age of thirty-five – the largest in the study. Gladys missed a great deal of schooling due to moving house to an isolated area in the Canadian Rockies, and was undoubtedly of weaker physique and poorer health than her more fortunate sister. Helen also lived on a farm in a fairly remote area but had a foster mother who, despite her husband's opposition to education for women, was determined that Helen should have the best opportunities. This resulted in her graduation from 'a good Michigan college' and a career in teaching. Newman concludes his comparisons of these sisters as follows: 'As an advertisement for a college education, the contrast between these twins should be quite effective' (p. 250).

Although Gladys and Helen certainly showed the biggest divergence both of test scores and of conditions of upbringing, other case histories reflect smaller but perhaps equally important variations. To pinpoint such differences with any degree of scientific accuracy is an almost impossible task; the most that can be achieved is rather crude ratings of environmental variations, such as those provided by social class indices. Using the Carr-Saunders and Jones ratings

(1937), Burt (1966) has argued that his own sample of fifty-three separated identical pairs were not selectively placed in foster homes comparable to those of the natural parents; in fact, his figures suggest that a disproportionately large number of placements occurs into working class families. Burt's study deliberately excluded twins who were brought up by other members of the family.

The number of separated identical pairs investigated by psychologists now amounts to about 100, but Burt is of the opinion that many more could be found if a more diligent search of local authority records were carried out by educational psychologists and others with access to children's departments' files. Larger numbers need to be studied because of the risk of social bias in the samples. We need to be sure that families who consent to their twins being separated do not represent an undue proportion of impoverished or 'problem' families who simply could not afford to look after two more infants. Examination of Burt's figures (1966) suggests that a disproportionate number of separated twins come from the lowest two occupational categories (thirty-two out of forty-seven, and another six in institutions); there may therefore be more substance than he admits in the criticism that because his separated twins do not come from 'the full range of the social and cultural scale', 'environmental differences have not had a fair opportunity to reveal themselves' (Halsey, 1959, cited by Burt, 1966). Burt argues that only a small number of the children were in private schools, but the skewed social distribution of his sample remains; on the other hand, the variance of his sample on IQ tests is comparable to that of the general population.

Another means of checking the effect of separation is to compare those separated within the first six months with those who were only separated after a year or more spent in the same environment. This was done by Vandenberg and Johnson (1968) who re-analysed data from all eight studies of separated pairs, including the original nineteen pairs studied by Newman. They report larger IQ differences for those who had been brought up together for a *longer* period than for those separated at an early age. The early separation group differed by an average of 5·5 IQ points, the late separation group by 9·59 points. The fact that similarity in IQ appears to be inversely related to the amount of time spent in a common environment is difficult to account for in terms of an environmental argument alone.

Further evidence along the same lines can be found in the study by Shields (1962), who compared forty-four MZ twins brought up together with forty-four pairs brought up apart; a small number of DZ pairs were also studied. Correlations for separated MZ pairs (0·77) were the same as for those brought up together (0·76) (The DZ correlation was 0·51). Vandenberg and Johnson (1968) also re-analysed Shields's data, comparing those separated before nine months, at or after one year of age, and a third group separated at birth but reunited between the ages of five and nine years. There were no significant differences in test scores between the three groups. Here again, a longer period of common early environment did not produce greater similarities in intelligence test scores.

The interpretation of intelligence test data for separated identical twins seems to depend partly on the orientation of the commentator. Those with a bias towards genetic interpretation emphasize the small or even non-existent differences when twins are separated, whereas those with an environmental bias place more weight on the decrease in within-pair similarities that occurs in at least some studies of separated twins. The first group can find more empirical support in data provided by Shields (1962) and Burt (1966), the second by turning to Newman's original correlations. Neither can find much satisfaction in the data, if they seriously question the sampling procedures and assumptions on which such studies are based. We need more convincing evidence that separated and unseparated identical pairs are comparable, and that the relative rarity of separated pairs may not mask other differences and characteristics.

Despite these difficulties, comparisons of separated and non-separated twins do reveal some fairly consistent trends, which cannot be explained away as sampling artefacts. These are conveniently illustrated by Jensen (1969) with a simple graph based on the median correlations reported by Erlenmeyer-Kimling and Jarvik (1963).

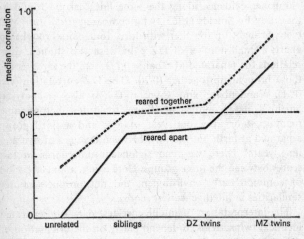

Figure 3 Median values of all correlations reported in the literature up to 1963 for the indicated kinships (after Erlenmeyer-Kimling and Jarvik, 1963). Note consistency of difference in correlations for relatives reared together and reared apart

Source: Jensen (1969)

The graph indicates that the extent of the differences between people brought up together and apart is very similar at all degrees of kinship. We can also compare heritability estimates based on MZ twins reared apart (0·75) with those based on unrelated children reared together (0·23). The proportion of the variance attributable to environment is around 25 per cent in both cases estimated independently. Jensen (1969) goes further by suggesting that we can also use this data to estimate environmental variance within and between families. His argument is quoted in full:

If $1.00 - 0.75$ (from MZ twins reared apart) estimates the total environmental variance, then $1.00 - 0.87 = 0.13$ (from MZ twins reared together) is an estimate of the environmental variance *within families* in which children are reared together. Thus the difference between $0.25 - 0.13 = 0.12$ is an estimate of the environmental variance *between families* (Jensen, 1969, p. 51).

We might expect, therefore, that if genetic factors play a relatively more important role in the development of intelligence, environmental factors exercise a more powerful influence on educational attainment. This conclusion is suggested by comparing results from intelligence and attainment tests. Burt's figures (1966) are shown in Table 7.

Table 7

Correlations for Intelligence and Attainments for Twins and Siblings

	MZ_t	MZ_a	DZ_t	Sibs
Intelligence (final assessment)	0·925	0·874	0·534	0·531
Attainments (general)	0·983	0·623	0·831	0·803
Reading and spelling	0·951	0·597	0·919	0·842
Arithmetic	0·862	0·705	0·748	0·754

Source: Burt (1966)

Further summaries of all twin studies of heritability of scholastic attainments are provided by Jensen (1969) whose conclusions are worth quoting in detail.

The analysis of all the twin studies on a variety of scholastic measures gives an average H of 0·40. The environmental variance of 60 per cent can be partitioned into variance due to environmental differences *between* families which is 54 per cent, and differences *within* families of 6 per cent. But it should also be noted that the heritability estimates for scholastic achievement vary over a much wider range than do *H* values for intelligence. In general, *H* for scholastic achievement increases as we go from the primary grades up to high school and it is somewhat lower for relatively simple forms of learning (e.g. spelling and arithmetic computation) than for more complex learning (e.g. reading comprehension and arithmetic problem solving). Yet large scale twin data from the National Merit Scholarship Corporation show that the *between families environmental* component accounts for about 60 per cent of the variance in students' rank in their high school graduating class. This must mean that there are strong family influences which cause children to conform to some academic standard set by the family and which reduce variance in scholastic performance among siblings reared in the same family ... *this means that there is much more that we can do to improve school performance through environmental means than we can do to change intelligence* per se (Jensen, 1969, pp. 58–9) [italics added].

Specific mental abilities

The distinctions made above between results of intelligence and attainment tests is an important one which has not in general been at all widely exploited in twin studies. Thus, most researchers have used general 'intelligence tests', yielding global IQs, which have then been used to compute correlations. We can now turn to the small number of studies which have attempted to examine specific cognitive functions from a genetic point of view. This is in line with current interest in isolating specific cognitive skills, and reflects a revival of interest in underlying constituent processes.

Probably the first twin study to attempt this kind of analysis was that of Blewett (1954) on London schoolchildren. He administered the Primary Abilities Test and the Nufferno Tests of Intellectual Level and Speed to twenty-six MZ and twenty-six DZ pairs, equally divided by sex. Blewett predicted that the second order factor derived from the primary abilities would represent predominantly hereditary influences. He also predicted, but could not confirm, that the heritability of the second order factor would be greater than that of the primary factors.

Table 8 tabulates Blewett's results for the components of the PMA battery – verbal, space, number, reasoning and fluency, and three composite scores.

Table 8

Intraclass Correlations of Thurstone's Primary
Mental Abilities and of Second-Order General Intelligence

PMA factor	Intraclass correlation		
	MZ	DZ	H
Verbal	0·726	0·145	0·680
Fluency	0·734	0·257	0·642
Reasoning	0·708	0·188	0·640
Space	0·630	0·248	0·508
Number	0·489	0·449	0·073
Composite II†	0·754	0·394	0·594
Composite III‡	0·732	0·406	0·549
Composite I*	0·583	0·369	0·339

* Composite I = PMA total by formula V+S+2R+W.

† Composite II = PMA total calculated as the square of Thurstone's second-order factor loadings.

‡ Composite III = PMA total score calculated on the basis of weights derived from Blewett's own group.

Source: Blewett (1954)

It is of interest that the number and space tests showed lower heritability estimates than the verbal and reasoning abilities. Blewett therefore speculates that perhaps 'good art students are born, whereas mathematicians, engineers and statisticians are made by training'.

If this conclusion were valid, it would clearly have important implications; a number of studies have subsequently repeated Blewett's work with the same test, but on various age groups. The main ones are those of Thurstone and Strandkov (1955) and two separate studies by the Louisville group (Vandenberg, 1962, 1965). Unfortunately, Koch (1966) who also used the PMA on ninety-six pairs of five- and six-year-old twins, presents intraclass correlations only for the PMA totals: these are 0·79 for MZs, 0·45 for DZSS and 0·52 for DZOS pairs, yielding an H of 0·62. Since we are mainly concerned with specific ability analyses in the present context, Koch's study will not be included in Table 9 which compares heritability estimates of the four

Table 9

Comparisons of Four Studies Estimating Heritability of Primary Mental Abilities

Ability	Blewett (1954)	Rank	Thurstone (1955)	Rank	Vandenberg (1962)	Rank	Vandenberg (1965)	Rank
Verbal	0·68	1	0·64	2	0·62	1	0·43	4
Reasoning	0·64	2	0·26	6	0·28	5	0·09	5
Word fluency	0·64	2	0·59	3	0·61	2	0·55	3
Space	0·51	4	0·76	1	0·59	4	0·72	1
Number	0·07	5	0·34	5	0·61	2	0·56	2
Memory			0·39	4	0·20	6		

Source: Vandenberg (1966)

studies quoted above: in all of these heritability is calculated by the Holzinger formula:

$$H = \frac{r_{MZ} - r_{DZ}}{1 - r_{DZ}}.$$

Comparison of these four studies reveals considerable differences when the heritabilities are placed in rank order, particularly in the case of number ability, which was very low in the English study, but higher for Vandenberg's studies. Conversely, Blewett obtained higher heritability values for reasoning. The discrepancies in these studies may be due to a number of reasons, including the failure of any of them to analyse their results separately for each sex. It is important in any study concerned with genetic factors to consider the role of sex differences in specific cognitive processes, particularly in language skills where sex differences are obviously relevant. All three American studies contained a very high proportion of female twins, whereas Blewett's sample was evenly balanced in this respect. It is also relevant to refer to evidence that the ability to visualize space is possibly a sex-linked recessive trait (Gottesman, 1963).

This account illustrates the problem of interpreting studies which have the same overall aim of making within-pair comparisons on specific abilities, but which result in somewhat different estimates of the degree to which one or other ability is accounted for by hereditary factors. It is rare for two studies to have exactly the same design or to use subjects of exactly the same age and background, and for this reason, it is in practice difficult to conduct cross-validational research in this field. Longitudinal studies would solve some of these difficulties. In the case of the Primary Mental Abilities, for example, it has been shown that the abilities isolated by the Thurstones for adults can be differentiated as early as five years (Meyers *et al.*, 1962).

Surprisingly enough, only one twin study using the Wechsler scales has been reported in the literature, despite the popularity of these scales and the considerable amount of normative data available on them. Block (1968), working in Vandenberg's laboratory, tested 120 pairs of adolescent twins, equally divided for sex and zygosity. Results were expressed in terms of the F-ratio for DZ and MZ within-pair variances, and also in terms of heritabilities (Holzinger's H).

Block's study (1968) can be criticized on a number of

Table 10

Comparison of Within-Pair Variances of Sixty D Z and Sixty M Z pairs on the Wechsler Adult Intelligence Scale

	F	H
Information	3·88‡	0·74
Comprehension	2·25†	0·55
Arithmetic	2·78‡	0·64
Similarities	1·81*	0·45
Digit Span	1·53*	0·35
Vocabulary	3·14‡	0·68
Digit Symbol	2·06†	0·51
Picture Completion	1·50	0·33
Block Design	2·35†	0·57
Picture Arrangement	1·74*	0·43
Object Assembly	1·36	0·26
Verbal IQ	3·38‡	0·70
Performance IQ	3·41‡	0·71
Full Scale IQ	3·47‡	0·71

$* p = 0·05$ $† p = 0·01$ $‡ p = 0·001$

Source: Block (1968)

grounds. In the first place, at least half of his subjects should have been given the Wechsler Intelligence Scale for Children, as they were under sixteen years old. Secondly, he had to use scaled scores rather than raw scores (since the subjects varied in age), thereby reducing the variance, since scaled scores range only between zero and nineteen; thirdly, we are not told whether the subjects were normally distributed on the tests, or how reliable the test results are; this is particularly important since many of his subjects must have had scores clustering near the lower end of the range and the validity of comparisons between sub-tests in this case is even further reduced when their reliability is low. It might even further have been preferable to restrict twin comparisons to each age group taken separately; this would have allowed him to use raw scores instead of scaled scores, and also to administer the more appropriate test. Nevertheless, the findings are of interest, since significant F-ratios are shown for all but two of the sub-tests, and verbal, performance and full-scale IQs show significance levels beyond the 0·001 level. A more detailed multivariate analysis is promised for a later publication.

Other cognitive abilities

In addition to work on specific intellectual abilities, a number of investigators have examined the heritability of other cognitive skills chiefly spatial, numerical and linguistic. A group of studies from the University of Georgia have compared M Z and D Z twins on a battery of spatial, numerical and verbal tests (Osborne and Gregor, 1966; Osborne, Gregor and Miele, 1967, 1968). The results reflect considerable variations in heritability estimates within each battery, but in almost every case M Z correlations were higher than D Z correlations. The tests used in these studies represent something of an *ad hoc* collection which have little obvious relationship to one another. Unlike Blewett's study (1954), no use was made of factor scores or of a composite test battery such as the P M A with some consistent structure or factorial composition. Nevertheless, the amount of agreement within each series of tests led the authors to conclude that the maximum extent of the genetic contribution to spatial, numerical and verbal abilities was 89, 72 and 78 per cent respectively. Their results are summarized in Table 11, together with the Holzinger estimate of heritability (H).

Further data on spatial and other cognitive tasks is provided by Vandenberg (1969), using some twins who were also tested in the Georgia Studies.

Vandenberg (1968b) reviews a number of other studies of specific abilities; these include his own work using the Differential Aptitude Battery, Wictorin's study (1952, cited by Vandenberg, 1968b) of a large number of Swedish twins

Table 11

Correlations, for Perceptual, Numerical and Verbal Tests, and Holzinger's H

	MZ ($N = 33$)	DZ ($N = 12$)	H
Perceptual			
Surface development 1	0·757	0·078	0·737
Surface development 2	0·873	0·183	0·845
Surface development total	0·911	0·197	0·889
Mazes	0·796	0·147	0·761
Newcastle Spatial Test	0·877	0·722	0·559
Paper folding	0·460	0·364	0·151
Identical pictures	0·710	0·262	0·602
Object aperture	0·685	0·483	0·391
Cube comparisons	0·698	0·527	0·361
Median of nine spatial tests	0·760	0·260	0·675
Arithmetic (in ascending order of difficulty)			
Part 1	0·461	0·573	−0·263
Part 2	0·774	0·202	0·717
Part 3	0·739	0·102	0·710
Part 4	0·818	0·625	0·515
Part 5	0·770	0·762	0·036
Part 6	0·720	0·167	0·664
Part 7	0·726	0·167	0·671
Arithmetic total	0·842	0·441	0·717
Vocabulary			
Heim self-judging vocabulary 1	0·449	0·059	0·415
Heim self-judging vocabulary 2	0·684	0·058	0·665
Heim self-judging vocabulary 3	0·579	−0·338	0·685
Heim self-judging vocabulary total	0·633	−0·133	0·676
Wide range vocabulary test	0·613	0·404	0·350
Heim self-judging vocabulary total	0·860	0·375	0·775
Spelling achievement	0·816	0·256	0·752
Median of seven verbal tests	0·630	0·060	0·606

Source: Osborne and Gregor (1966); Osborne, Gregor and Miele (1967, 1968); Vandenberg (1969b)

using a psychological test battery, a similar Finnish study by Bruun, Markanen and Partanen (1966) using eight tests of five primary mental abilities and Husén's study (1953) of attainment and intelligence tests in Swedish twins. All of these studies show consistently larger within-pair variances in DZ than in MZ twins, but the extent of the genetic contribution obviously varies considerably: moreover, most of these studies can be criticized for using an arbitrary assemblage of tests, unrelated to a consistent or satisfactory model of intellectual ability. Quite often, the reliability of the measures is not stated.

Language

A study of psycholinguistic abilities has been reported by the writer using the Illinois Test of Psycholinguistic Abilities (Mittler, 1969b). This test which is based on a model of language behaviour developed by Osgood (1957) claims to assess nine separate and distinct aspects of psycholinguistic functioning, though factorial studies suggest that at least 40 per cent of the variance of the test may be accounted for by a general linguistic factor (Mittler and Ward, 1970). As a result of testing twenty-eight MZ and sixty-four DZ pairs of forty-eight-month-old twins on the ITPA, it was suggested that between 44 per cent and 69 per cent of the variance of the total ITPA score was genetic in origin, but that the extent of the genetic contribution to specific psycholinguistic abilities varied considerably. For example, heritabilities were higher for the visual-motor than for the auditory-vocal channel, and also for tests not requiring speech from the subject. This is consistent with findings from other studies suggesting that non-verbal tests may have higher heritabilities than verbal tests, and is indirectly confirmed by other work with the ITPA indicating that social class is more strongly associated with scores on the auditory-vocal than on the visual-motor channel (Teasdale and Katz, 1968; Weaver and Weaver, 1967). In our own study, the Seguin Form Board also showed higher heritabilities (62 per cent) than the Peabody Picture Vocabulary Test (36 per cent). The ITPA findings are summarized in Table 12.

Table 12

Correlations for the Illinois Test of Psycholinguistic Abilities from Four-Year-Old Twins

ITPA sub-tests	MZ (N = 28 pairs)	DZ (N = 64 pairs)	H	h^2
Auditory decoding	0·52	0·72	−0·714	−0·40
Visual decoding	0·74	0·24	0·658	1·00
Auditory-vocal association	0·81	0·68	0·406	0·26
Visual-motor association	0·78	0·15	0·741	1·26
Vocal encoding	0·63	0·43	0·351	0·40
Motor encoding	0·66	0·35	0·477	0·62
Auditory-vocal automatic	0·82	0·55	0·600	0·54
Auditory-vocal sequential	0·56	0·49	0·137	0·14
Visual-motor sequential	0·46	0·49	−0·060	0·06
ITPA total	0·90	0·68	0·687	0·44

Source: Mittler (1969b)

The occasional appearance of 'impossible' H or h^2 values will be noted in these studies. It is, of course, theoretically impossible for heritability values to be negative, or to exceed unity. Nevertheless, such ratios may be found and are due to unreliability of the tests and of the subjects. This is the price to be paid for attempts to measure specific cognitive abilities by tests such as Primary Mental Abilities, and batteries of spatial, numerical or psycholinguistic measures.

Conclusions

Individual differences in human intelligence are to a substantial extent attributable to genetic factors. This conclusion follows inescapably from an examination of the voluminous literature dealing not only with twins, but also with other pedigree and family studies including some examining the effect of inbreeding on intelligence of adopted and foster children, and of children brought up in different environments. Such a conclusion may be unacceptable at a time when 'fashions' in psychology and education emphasize the role of environment in the development of intelligence: but it would be wrong to dichotomize the environmental and genetic arguments as though they were mutually exclusive. No one believes that genetic 'instructions' for the development of, say, high intelligence develop in an environmental vacuum: it is an axiom of biology that an appropriate environment is necessary for the full expression of many genetically determined characteristics, particularly those influenced by polygenic modes of inheritance, as opposed to others such as eye colour. Similarly, no one would deny that precise determination of the extent of genetic contribution is fraught with all kinds of difficulties, though the attempt may nevertheless be worth making. It is also generally recognized that hereditary and environmental factors interact in the individual, but the interaction is perhaps not so complex as to be impossible to unravel.

The case for a substantial genetic contribution to intelligence is accepted by many psychologists, partly because the evidence, though certainly open to criticism on methodological and other grounds, is on the whole impressively consistent, and partly because there is no necessary contradiction between accepting the genetic case (albeit, with strong reservations) and still emphasizing the role of environmental variables. An appreciation of the importance of the genetic contribution to intelligence by no means justifies a passive inertia about the possibilities of environmental attempts to make better use of human intellectual resources. The fact that a particular ability or skill may be largely genetic in origin should not make teachers pessimistic about their efforts, partly because a substantial portion of the variance is still environmental in origin, and partly because it is not so much 'intelligence' as the *use* of intelligence with which we are concerned in everyday life. No one has ever claimed that we are in sight of raising Intelligence A (to use Hebb's well-known distinction (1949)) since this is essentially physiological and genetic in origin; the best that we can do is help the child to make more effective use of his abilities and to help him acquire the necessary knowledge and skills to enable him to function as near as possible to his potential, even though we cannot determine at all precisely what that potential might be in any given case. In other words, teaching and other environmental measures can do much to modify Intelligence B – the use to which intelligence is put in living – because this is partly a matter of knowledge and skills, and because it is profoundly affected by factors such as motivation, parental attitudes and the presence of a facilitating and encouraging environment.

Moreover, teachers should not need to be as concerned with intelligence as with educational achievement – and here, as we have tried to show, the evidence from twins and from other sources indicates quite clearly that environmental factors play a much stronger part in determining educational achievement than can be demonstrated in the case of intelligence tests. Separated identical twins show considerable disparities in their educational achievements, even though their IQs may be very similar; fraternal twins brought up together show higher correlations for educational than for intelligence tests.

The preoccupation of psychologists and some educationalists with the IQ is also reflected in the current controversies over attempts to provide compensatory education for disadvantaged pre-schoolchildren. These 'head start', and similar programmes, have not, with a few exceptions, been in operation long enough to be properly evaluated, but preliminary results have not been altogether encouraging. It is ironical, however, that the very people who criticize the IQ as insensitive or as culturally biased, are often those who use IQ tests to measure the effectiveness of a compensatory education programme. By this criterion, the programmes have not so far been shown to be a marked success. Jensen (1969) reviews a large number of reports, and shows how IQ rises have often been minimal and statistically insignificant, and that where control groups have been used, they have sometimes shown bigger IQ rises than the experimental group. This controversy is mentioned here, because it illustrates the belief, widely prevalent in psychological and educational circles, that special educational measures to help children with learning difficulties should result in the raising of intellectual ability, as measured by IQ.

If performance on such tests is influenced by genetic variables, we should not expect dramatic IQ rises as a result of intervention programmes, though there is no reason why educational attainments should not be substantially affected. Indeed, there is evidence that results have been more positive where the programmes have concentrated on specific cognitive skills, especially those involving aspects of language (Bereiter and Engelmann, 1966). Such attempts to improve specific verbal abilities can also be justified on the grounds that they have been shown to be related to environmental variables, particularly to social class and the child's linguistic background (Bernstein, 1965).

We must conclude, therefore, that a consideration of the scientific evidence from twin studies and from other sources can leave little doubt of the importance of genetic sources of individual differences in intelligence, as conventionally measured. Such findings should be placed in the broader biological perspective of work in behaviour genetics which has concerned itself with traits other than intelligence – for example, variables such as sensory and motor behaviour and complex responses considered in previous chapters. Although human intelligence and the influences that affect its development are exceedingly complex, there is no reason why man should mark a sharp discontinuity in evolution, and turn out to be totally immune from the workings of genetic processes which affect lower organisms. The interactions between his genetic endowment and the experiences derived from learning are infinitely more complex, chiefly because he can reflect on his own experience through his use of language and symbols. Moreover, man can act purposefully to modify and enrich his environment and try to counter those genetic influences which he considers injurious. This he has been partially successful in doing – as in the case of genetically determined disorders such as phenylketonuria. Much remains to be done in this field – attempts to prevent chromosome disorders such as Down's Disease are an obvious example – but much more might be done to remove those barriers to learning and to the use of intellectual skills which stem from defective environments.

6 Personality

Despite the predominant interest in intelligence of most twin studies, there has recently been a growing emphasis on personality. This is partly due to the increasing use of more objective personality tests, which were not available to previous investigators, and partly to the realization that cognitive and non-cognitive factors should be thought of as interacting rather than as distinct. The use of multifactorial tests has tended to focus interest on specific aspects of personality, rather than on personality as a whole; viewed in this light, genetic factors can be shown to play a significant part in personality functioning, but their influence is more obvious for some aspects of personality than others. The difficulties lie in definition and measurement.

Definitions of personality as an overall, global construct tend to stress its organizational aspects; on this view, intelligence is just one aspect of personality. For example, Griffiths defines personality as 'the more or less stable organization of a person's emotional, cognitive, intellectual and conceptual, and physiological behaviour which determines to a large extent his adjustments to environmental situations' (1970, p. 83).

Considerable advances are now taking place in assessment, and in the production of reasonably reliable and valid tests of personality; this is undoubtedly one of the factors contributing to renewed attempts to estimate genetic components of personality functioning. It may be convenient to trace the development of interest in this field from its earliest origins, while illustrating some of the more serious methodological problems involved.

The first important twin study using personality tests was

that of Newman, Freeman and Holzinger (1937), whose findings in respect of intelligence tests were quoted earlier. Newman used a number of tests which would not now be thought adequate for the purposes of personality assessment, but reported important findings, some of which have been confirmed by later workers. He provides full details of his results on the Woodworth–Mathews Personality Inventory (a test of neurotic tendencies) for identical twins brought up both together and apart, together with comparisons between identical and fraternal twins for the Downey Will–Temperament Test. The results are summarized in Table 13, which also includes an estimate of Holzinger's H, computed for the purpose of this review by the usual formula.[1]

$$H = \frac{r_{MZ} - r_{DZ}}{1 - r_{DZ}}.$$

The Newman data seem to reflect a moderate genetic component in respect of the Woodworth–Mathews test, in so far as the MZ correlations (0·56) are higher than the DZ correlations (0·37), and because the separated identicals were no different from those brought up together. On the other hand, the Downey tests reflect only environmental influences, since the DZ correlations are in three cases out of four higher than those for MZs. Newman concluded that none of the personality tests reflected any genetic influences, and attributed the higher correlations for separated identicals on the Woodworth tests to unreliability; nevertheless, this finding has been repeatedly confirmed, as we shall see. However, Eysenck (1967) criticizes this study not only because the data do not support the

---

1. Alternatively, where only within-pair variances are given for other tables in this chapter,

$$H = \frac{v_{DZ} - v_{MZ}}{v_{DZ}}.$$

Similarly, the F- or variance-ratio v_{DZ}/v_{MZ} may be tested for significance by consulting the appropriate tables.

Table 13

Correlations and Heritabilities (H) for Personality Tests from Chicago Twin Study

	MZ$_t$ (N = 50)	MZ$_a$ (N = 19)	DZ (N = 50)	H
Woodworth–Mathews Personality Inventory	0·56	0·58	0·37	0·30
Downey Will–Temperament Test				
Speed of decision	0·50		0·69	
Finality of judgement	0·31		0·37	
Motor inhibition	0·51		0·37	
Coordination of impulses	0·82		0·79	0·14

Source: Newman, Freeman and Holzinger (1937)

conclusions drawn, but also because tests designed for adults were administered to children. Similar criticisms apply to other early studies (e.g. Carter, 1933). These early studies also labour under the disadvantage of using tests of unknown or poor reliability and validity, and generally lacking in any coherent theoretical rationale. The items often consist of 'common sense' questions loosely relating to adjustment, anxiety or the presence of certain symptoms of neurosis or maladjustment.

An alternative approach is to use tests which are deliberately designed to be multifactorial, and which include scales purporting to measure specific personality traits. Examples of such tests are the Minnesota Multiphasic Personality Inventory (MMPI) and the California Personality Inventory (CPI). Some examples of recent twin studies will serve to illustrate the approach.

Gottesman used the MMPI in two studies (1963, 1965), one conducted on thirty-four MZ and thirty-four DZ adolescent twin pairs in Minneapolis, with a high proportion of subjects of Scandinavian origin, and the other on eighty-two MZ and sixty-eight DZ pairs in Boston, Massachusetts. The results of the two studies were not consistent, suggesting that variables connected with population genetics may provide greater complexities in the interpretation of data collected from different ethnic groups. Inconsistencies are also attributable to age, since there is no reason why personality tests and twin correlations obtained from children should be similar to those found for adults.

Table 14

Heritabilities (H) and F-ratios Derived from MMPI

	1963			1965		
	H	F	Rank	H	F	Rank
Hypochondriasis	0·16	1·19	7	0·01	1·01	10
Depression	0·45	1·82*	3	0·45	1·82*	1
Hysteria	0·00	0·86	10	0·30	1·43	7
Psychopathy	0·50	2·01*	2	0·39	1·63*	2
Masculinity/ femininity	0·15	1·18	8	0·29	1·41	8
Paranoia	0·05	1·05	9	0·38	1·61*	3
Psychasthenia	0·37	1·58	5	0·31	1·46	6
Schizophrenia	0·42	1·71	4	0·33	1·49*	4
Hypomania	0·24	1·32	6	0·13	1·15	9
Social introversion	0·71	3·42*	1	0·33	1·49*	4

* $p = 0.05$

Source: Gottesman (1963, 1965)

The MMPI consists of 550 questions which yield scores on ten aspects of personality. Gottesman's results, together with estimates of Holzinger's H, may be compared in Table 14.

If the heritability values of the two Gottesman studies are

placed in rank order, it will be seen that reasonable agreement exists between them, with the exception of paranoia. For the purpose of the present discussion, a Spearman rank order correlation was calculated, resulting in a ρ of 0·5 for all ten scales, which just fails to reach significance. In general, however, the data suggest that higher heritabilities were found for social introversion and psychopathy, and also for the two 'psychotic' scales (depression and schizophrenia). Eysenck (1967) interprets these findings in terms of support for a positive genetic contribution to extraversion–introversion which he associates with scales labelled social introversion, psychopathy, psychasthenia and, to a lesser degree, hysteria.

Consideration of these findings from the MMPI illustrates the complexities of interpretation involved. Although some measure of consistency appears to be present, results may be shown to vary according to the age and sex of the subjects, and the geographical area where the study is conducted.

As part of the same Boston study, Gottesman (1966) used the California Personality Inventory (CPI) (Gough, 1965) with seventy-nine MZ pairs (thirty-four male, forty-five female) and sixty-eight DZ pairs (thirty-two male, thirty-six female). The twins were between ninth and twelfth grade (i.e. in mid to late adolescence). The CPI is described by Gough as 'a true–false objective inventory scaled for "folk concepts", that is variables used for the description and analysis of personality in everyday life and in social interaction' (Gough, 1965, cited by Gottesman, 1966). The twins were carefully blood typed to ensure accurate zygosity determination; the sample was recruited from school registers and also, where this proved impossible, through advertising and clubs for mothers of twins: it was somewhat biased towards middle class and professional families, and also because unreliable or invalid records (as determined by high 'L' or 'F' scores on the MMPI) had to be discarded, thereby restricting the intelligence and possibly the personality range of the group. The particular interest of this study relates not only to its findings as such, but to its methodology. Most of the studies considered so far have confined themselves to measurement of actual test scores or scales; the present study, and others to be described later, have considered factor scores. This technique has been shown to be of great value in examining batteries of intelligence tests (Blewett, 1954; see also chapter 5); its extension to the personality field is long overdue. Gottesman (1966) bases his analysis on a factor analytic study of the CPI reported by Nichols and Schnell (1963), who found that two main factors accounted for most of the variance of the test; these were labelled person orientation and value orientation. Gottesman (1966) prefers to rename them extraversion–introversion and dependability–undependability respectively, presumably in order to bring them into line with Eysenck's model of personality. Table 15 summarizes heritability and significance data in relation to these factors.

The first factor scale correlated -0.66 with the Social Introversion scale of the MMPI, and can reasonably be regarded as an extraversion–introversion scale. It is apparent that around 50 per cent of the variance is accounted for by genetic factors on this scale, in contrast to the substantially lower proportion on the dependability–undependability factor. Unfortunately, Gottesman does not report data for the factor score *per se*, as Blewett (1954) and others have done for Primary Mental Abilities and similar multifactorial tests.

In fact, the first study to use factor scores was one by Eysenck and Prell (1951). They criticized tests based on single measures, and argued that heritability should be calculated only from those tests having the highest loadings on the general factors of neuroticism or extraversion. They point out, moreover, that objective tests of behaviour are superior to personality questionnaires, especially when children are the subjects, and are less subject to faking. Finally, they suggest that the factor scores should themselves be validated wherever possible against an external

Table 15

Heritability of Factor Scores Derived from California
Personality Inventory

Cluster	CPI scale	H	F
Factor I			
Person orientation or	Sociability	0·49	1·97†
extraversion–introversion	Self acceptance	0·46	1·85*
	Social presence	0·35	1·55*
	Dominance	0·49	1·95†
Factor II			
Value orientation or	Responsibility	0·26	1·35
dependability–undependability	Socialization	0·32	1·48*
	Self-control	0·27	1·38
	Tolerance	0·27	1·37
	Good impression	0·38	1·60*
	Communality	0·19	1·23

* $p = 0·05$
† $p = 0·01$

Source: Gottesman (1966)

criterion; for example by indicating, as they did in a
separate study, that children under treatment at a child
guidance clinic could be clearly differentiated on factor
scores of neuroticism from normal controls (Eysenck and
Prell, 1951). In a later study, Eysenck (1956) reported more
factor data on extraversion, autonomic activity and intelligence. The results of these studies are summarized in Table
16.

The most recent developments of Eysenck's work on
personality measurement are incorporated in the Eysenck
Personality Inventory, but only one twin study using this
test has been tentatively reported. This forms part of the
Glasgow twin project, by Claridge and his associates (in
press), whose work in connection with sedation threshold and

psycho-physiological indices was discussed in chapter 4. A preliminary account of work on personality was reported by Canter (1969), but full details have not yet been published. Eighty-five pairs of adolescent and adult twins were tested on the Eysenck Personality Inventory, a Sociability and Impulsivity Scale (also based on the EPI), Cattell's sixteen PF scale, and Foulds's Hostility Scale. The subjects

Table 16

Intraclass Correlations and Heritability Derived from Factor Scores of Neuroticism, Extraversion and Autonomic Activity

	MZ	DZ	*H*
Eysenck and Prell (1951)			
Neuroticism	0·85	0·22	0·81
Eysenck (1956)			
Extraversion	0·50	−0·33	0·62
Autonomic activity	0·93	0·72	0·75
Intelligence	0·82	0·38	0·71

were volunteers, and were, as usual, biased by the inclusion of a disproportionate number of young, intelligent middle class females. These sampling biases are not uncommon in twin research, but they do seem particularly marked in the Glasgow subjects. The EPI data are summarized in Table 17.

The data reflect low heritabilities on both neuroticism and extraversion, but higher scores on sociability and possibly impulsivity; the negative correlation for the DZ twins casts some doubt on the reliability of the impulsivity scale. It is apparent, however, that these results hold only for the females.

Canter has presented some interesting data comparing

both MZ and DZ twins who had been separated for more than five years with those separated for less than five years. The data are also summarized in Table 17. She concludes

Table 17

Within Pair Variances and Heritabilities of Eysenck Personality Inventory

	Correlations			
	Neuroticism	Extra-version	Socia-bility	Impulsivity
MZ ($N = 40$)	0·37	0·34	0·67	0·24
DZ ($N = 45$)	0·23	0·29	0·25	−0·03
Heritability	0·18	0·07	0·56	0·26
	F-Ratios			
Male ($N = 23$)	2·27	0·93	1·21	0·99
Female ($N = 62$)	1·23	1·06	2·78†	2·29*
Total ($N = 85$)	1·41	0·99	2·32†	1·84*
	Correlations			
MZ$_t$ ($N = 25$)	0·53	0·10	0·51	−0·03
MZ$_a$ ($N = 15$)	0·18	0·67	0·91	0·20
DZ$_t$ ($N = 29$)	0·70	0·22	0·25	−0·26
DZ$_a$ ($N = 16$)	−0·17	0·36	0·25	0·35

* $p < 0.05$
† $p < 0.01$

Source: Canter (1969)

that on measures of neuroticism, all twin pairs, whether MZ or DZ, are more alike when together or recently separated, and become less alike when separated for more than five years. This is particularly true of DZ pairs. However, the reverse is true on measures of extraversion, sociability and impulsivity; separated twins are more alike than those brought up together. In general, however, her results indicate a substantial genetic factor for extraversion, and for sociability in particular, as measured by the EPI.

Canter also reports some interesting results on Cattell's sixteen PF test. This is perhaps the most ambitious example of a test developed entirely in terms of its factorial structure. It has been widely used by Cattell's own group at Illinois to investigate family resemblances in personality traits by the use of the MAVA method (multiple abstract variance analysis). Its rationale is lucidly expounded in Cattell's book *The Scientific Analysis of Personality* (1965b), and examples of the method applied to twin and family data can be found in a large number of his publications (e.g. 1965a). Table 18 summarizes Canter's data for each of the sixteen scales, and also for the three second-order factors – neuroticism, anxiety and extraversion (reproduced by kind permission of Mrs Sandra Canter from unpublished material). Once again, H has been specially computed from the correlations; F-ratios are provided by Canter.

The data resulted in moderate H values on factors A, H, I, L, O and Q_2, and in addition significant F-ratios on factor B. The second-order factors, while leading to insignificant F-ratios, nevertheless suggest that genetic factors account for about 30 per cent of the variance. More detailed analyses of the data provided by Canter, but not reproduced here, emphasize the importance of sex differences in the analysis of personality data, though the differences may in the case of this study be due to the small sample of male twins. In particular, F-ratios were much higher in males for placidity and in females for toughmindedness and trust.

Canter's comparisons between separated and non-separated twins yielded similar results for the sixteen PF as for the EPI, and are generally in line with studies by Shields (1962) and Wilde (1964). Relying entirely on volunteers recruited from a television appeal, Shields (1962) compared forty-four pairs of MZ pairs brought up apart with forty-four pairs brought up together: the two samples were reason-

Table 18

Correlations, Heritabilities and F-Ratios for Cattell's Sixteen Personality Factor Test, Derived from Glasgow Twin Project

Factor	Name	r_{MZ}	r_{DZ}	H	F
A	Reserved v. outgoing	0·49	0·29	0·35	1·02
B	Less intelligent v. more intelligent	0·23	0·13	0·12	1·84*
C	Affected by feeling v. emotionally stable	0·37	0·15	0·26	1·03
E	Humble v. assertive	0·27	0·30		1·10
F	Sober v. happy-go-lucky	0·56	0·47	0·17	0·98
G	Expedient v. conscientious	0·14	0·34		0·77
H	Shy v. venturesome	0·58	0·30	0·40	1·48
I	Tough-minded v. tender-minded	0·68	0·25	0·57	2·89†
L	Trusting v. suspicious	0·34	0·05	0·31	1·74*
M	Practical v. imaginative	0·23	0·08	0·16	1·47
N	Forthright v. shrewd	0·19	0·30		0·84
O	Placid v. apprehensive	0·38	0·06	0·34	1·89*
Q_1	Conservative v. experimenting	0·25	0·09	0·18	0·89
Q_2	Group dependent v. self-sufficient	0·39	0·01	0·38	1·26
Q_3	Undisciplined self-conflict v. controlled	0·22	0·23		0·80
Q_4	Relaxed v. tense	0·20	0·10	0·11	0·77

Second-order factors					
Neuroticism		0·36	0·06	0·32	1·30
Extraversion		0·56	0·33	0·36	1·36
Anxiety		0·43	0·08	0·38	1·34

* $p < 0.05$
† $p < 0.01$

Source: Canter (1969)

ably matched for age and sex, but both contained an unduly high proportion of women in their thirties and forties. In addition, twenty-eight DZ pairs brought up together were investigated, though in less detail. His results for intelligence tests were summarized in the previous chapter, and those for personality are now shown in Table 19. Shields used an early version of the Maudsley Personality Inventory which was

Table 19

Mean Intra-Pair Differences in Extraversion and Neuroticism of MZ Twins Brought Up Together and Apart and DZ Twins

	Extraversion		Neuroticism	
	Intra-pair difference	Correlation	Intra-pair difference	Correlation
MZ$_t$ (N = 43)	2·71	0·42	2·97	0·38
MZ$_a$ (N = 42)	2·52	0·61	3·10	0·53
DZ (N = 25)	4·72	−0·17	4·04	0·11
H		0·50		0·30

Source: Shields (1962)

specially devised for his investigation by Eysenck 'from the results of Guildford's factor analysis of many hundreds of questionnaire items so as to yield the greatest amount of discrimination compatible with its shortness' (Shields, 1962, p. 66). The tests consist of thirty-eight items, of which twenty-two contribute to extraversion and another twenty-two to neuroticism, with six items common to both. There is little information on reliability or validity, though these are reported to be comparable to the MPI and later EPI (Eysenck, personal communication).

As far as extraversion is concerned, Shields's data provides some confirmation of the strength of genetic factors: the difference between the MZ twins brought up together (0·42) and the DZ group (−0·17) yields a Holzinger H of 0·50: on the other hand, the absence of any relationship within DZ pairs, as reflected in a negative correlation, again casts doubt on the reliability of the measure. However, the most striking finding concerns the higher correlation for separated identicals (0·61) compared with those brought up together (0·42). Similar, though weaker, tendencies in the same direction are reflected in the neuroticism data. Here, H is only 0·30, though correlation for separated twins is again higher (0·53) than for those brought up together (0·38). However, the intra-pair differences do not quite give the same impression as the correlations, so that the suspicion of a statistical artefact cannot be altogether discounted. Similarly, Shields himself makes it clear that the two groups of identicals are not strictly comparable, and may come from different populations, statistically speaking. More specifically, the separated twins are somewhat less intelligent, and of 'poorer personality'. There were in many cases special circumstances associated with the separation, which make it difficult to compare the separated twins with others. Nevertheless, the study, though far from conclusive, represents an important contribution which has been independently confirmed by other workers, particularly by Wilde (1964) in a study carried out in Holland.

Wilde examined eighty-eight MZ and forty-two DZ pairs, of whom eleven pairs were opposite sex pairs; the sample was again biased by the inclusion of a disproportionate number of young women. The Amsterdam Biographical Questionnaire which was used in this study consists of 107 items measuring the following traits:

1. N, or neurotic instability as manifested by the presence of psychoneurotic complaints.

2. NS, or neurotic instability as manifested by the presence of functional bodily complaints, such as headaches, palpitations, blurred vision.

3. E, or extraversion,

4. T, or test-taking attitude (self-critical *v.* defensive; lie score).

The test has been standardized on nearly 2000 Dutch subjects between the ages of thirteen and seventy-eight; N and NS scores are reported to show reasonable validity against external criteria.

Wilde divided both the MZ and DZ pairs into those who had been living separately for more than five years, and those who were living together or who had been separated for less than five years. Although this division produced reasonable subgroups from a statistical point of view, one could argue that the effect of a five-year separation is likely to depend on the age of the subject; thus, a pair of twins separated between birth and six years is not likely to be comparable to another pair who lived together until their

Table 20

Correlations and Heritabilities (*H*) Derived from Amsterdam Biographical Questionnaire

		N	NS	E	T
MZt	(*N* = 50)	0·55	0·46	0·58	0·48
MZa	(*N* = 38)	0·52	0·75	0·19	0·46
MZ total	(*N* = 88)	0·53	0·67	0·37	0·46
DZt	(*N* = 21)	−0·14	−0·05	0·19	0·33
DZa	(*N* = 21)	0·28	0·64	0·36	0·49
DZ total	(*N* = 42)	0·11	0·34	0·35	0·54
H		0·50	0·18	0·35	

Source: Wilde (1964)

twenties, and were only tested after a further twenty years of separation. Wilde's results are reproduced in Table 20.

Comparing first the correlations for all MZ with those for all DZ twins, it can be seen that the highest heritability is found for N (0·50) and E (0·35), followed by NS (0·18). T appears to be unaffected by genetic influences in the light of these figures. Secondly, it is apparent that separated twins have either very similar correlations, in the case of N, or substantially higher correlations, in the case of NS, than those brought up together. The same tendency is seen to a smaller degree in respect of extraversion, but for DZ pairs only. Here again, it would not be predicted on a genetic hypothesis that DZ twins would show low, insignificant or even negative correlations; nor would one expect separated MZ pairs to show lower correlations than separated DZ pairs, as in the E scores. Nevertheless, the results are reasonably consistent with the studies reviewed earlier.

Evidence from longitudinal studies

It can probably be concluded from the evidence reviewed so far that some aspects of personality, particularly the extraversion–introversion dimension, consistently reflect greater similarities within identical than within fraternal pairs, and that this relationship is on occasion still present even when the twins have lived in different environments. But evidence for the contribution of genetic factors to this or other aspects of personality need not be sought in twin studies alone. In a recent review, Scarr (1969) makes the important point that the high consistency for social extraversion–introversion which has been found in several longitudinal studies on single children might in fact be explained by the heritability of this trait. She tabulates data from the well-known studies by Kagan and Moss (1962) and Schaeffer and Bayley (1963) who obtained comparable results from different samples and different tests; in both cases the authors reported substantial consistency on ratings of individual differences in social behaviour from infancy to adolescence. In general, consistency was higher for boys than for girls; in the former, 'social anxiety and friendliness in adolescence could be predicted during the first year of life, whereas for girls individual differences were consistent from early school age' (Scarr, 1969, p. 829).

Other longitudinal studies not specifically concerned with the extraversion–introversion dimension could also be invoked at this point. In a study carried out some time ago, Neilon (1948) showed that judges could identify adolescents at eighteen years from personality descriptions which were written when the subjects were two years old. A more ambitious longitudinal study is being reported by Birch and his associates (Thomas *et al.*, 1964), who find substantial long-term consistency in personality organization from the first few months of life. They obtained ratings of behaviour clusters under such headings as adaptability, rhythmicity, response threshold, attention span and persistence, and found that although there were wide individual differences between children, each child was remarkably consistent with himself. The same conclusion might also be reached on the basis of the many studies now available of the behaviour and responsiveness of newborn infants to a wide range of experimental situations. The Birch studies have been carried out for the most part on normal singletons, but a subsample of twins was studied by Rutter, Korn and Birch (1962), who reported much higher concordance of MZ than DZ twins on the main personality clusters.

A further source of evidence comes from the work of Shaffer and Emerson (1964, Shaffer, 1965) who in a series of observational studies have stressed the wide individual differences shown by a group of babies in respect of the strength of their social attachments (see also Freedman (1965) for a twin study of smiling and social development). In other words, they confirm what most mothers have always known, that some babies can be categorized as 'cuddlers' and others as 'non-cuddlers'; their data did not indicate any obvious relationship between cuddliness and the way in which the mothers handled the babies, though they did show marked similarities between siblings within a single family. Gottesman (1966) goes further in speculating on the possible polygenic system that may underlie the extraversion–introversion dimension, and argues that absence of some of the appropriate genes may be associated with pathological 'non-attachment' systems, such as those seen in infantile autism.

Finally, reference must be made to Eysenck's (1967a) comprehensive discussion of the biological foundations of personality. His discussion of these questions is too lengthy to

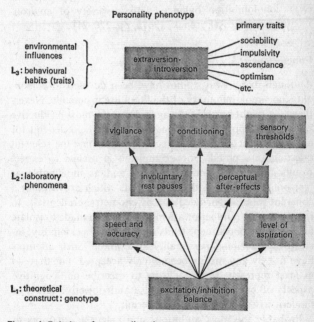

Figure 4 Relation of personality phenotype to genotype and environment

be adequately summarized, but he does draw a useful distinction between three levels of functioning. These are illustrated diagrammatically in Figure 4.

At the lowest level, lies the theoretical construct of the

excitation–inhibition balance – i.e. 'the relative predomin-
ance of excitatory or inhibitory potential in different people'.
This allows certain predictions to be made of the behaviour
of an individual at the second level, which is concerned with
phenomena that are usually assessed in the laboratory:
speed, vigilance, involuntary rest pauses, conditioning, etc.
Eysenck argues that 'primary traits such as sociability, impulsivity, ascendance, optimism and so on, which combine
to make up our phenotypic concept of extraversion, arise
through the confluence of a person's genotype, i.e. his
excitation–inhibition balance, with a variety of environmental influences' (Eysenck, 1967a, pp. 220–21).

Conclusions

Although many twin studies have been devoted to personality, no simple summary of the literature is possible. Nevertheless, it might be generally agreed that the most productive
attempts to apply the twin method in this field depend for
any limited success on the precision with which the relevant
questions are posed. For example, it is useless to expect
results from constructs as general and as indefinable as
'personality', or from the use of tests which are without a
coherent rationale or adequate psychometric credentials. In
recent years, a number of attempts have been made to isolate
and examine constituent traits or aspects of personality, instead of describing personality as a whole. Such attempts
have not by any means been widely accepted, but they do
at least represent serious efforts to describe non-cognitive
aspects of behaviour in as precise and objective terms as
modern assessment techniques permit.

Probably the most ambitious and extensive attempts to
provide both a viable model of personality and an adequate
assessment technique can be seen in the work of Eysenck and
Cattell; Eysenck's model consists of two higher-order independent factors (neuroticism and extraversion–introversion),
and Cattell's studies resulted in sixteen first-order factors.
Eysenck's system is of particular interest to the biologically

oriented psychologist, since its more recent developments have included attempts to relate personality functioning to constitutional variables such as conditionability, speed of cognitive functioning, body type, etc. (e.g. Eysenck, 1967b). Whatever the limitations of such a model from a theoretical or methodological point of view, it is obviously of particular interest to the student of human behaviour genetics, and Eysenck himself has provided some relevant information. Although the information yielded by twin studies is by no means consistent, the results reviewed in this chapter do give some support to the hypothesis of a moderate genetic contribution to extraversion. The data for neuroticism point in the same direction, though less convincingly.

If extraversion does indeed involve a substantial genetic factor, then it is obviously important to look at sources other than twin studies for evidence which might have a bearing on this question. One source of such evidence lies in the data available in longitudinal studies, which have consistently indicated long-term stability ratings of social behaviour from early childhood to maturity, especially for boys. In fact, a number of studies have drawn attention to the possibility of a greater degree of consistency in at least some aspects of personality organization than has perhaps been allowed in the past.

It cannot be too strongly stressed that despite the variance which is attributable to genetic factors, environmental factors still play an important part. Moreover, it should be obvious that statements about the relative contribution of heredity or environment refer only to specific populations and cannot be extrapolated to individuals or to other groups in the form of a general psychobiological law. Other populations tested under different conditions and with different tests may well produce different heritability ratios, partly for reasons of sampling, but also because most of the currently available tests are highly imperfect. However, at a time when environmental factors are receiving a great deal of attention, it does seem worth while to stress that genetic factors cannot be discounted in any discussion of personality development, and may be more important than is generally admitted. The task that now awaits psychologists is that of studying the ongoing interaction between genetic and environmental factors, in the hope of gaining some measure of understanding not so much of the relative contribution of one or other set of variables, but of the actual processes and mechanisms involved. Because of our relative ignorance of these mechanisms, statements about the contribution of 'nature' or 'nurture' must be treated with caution and a sense of relevance.

7 Mental Disorders

The scientific examination of genetic factors in mental illness is exceedingly complex. Although a very large number of studies have been devoted to this question, and although there can be no doubt that genetic factors have time and again been shown to be of considerable importance, the role of environmental factors should not be underestimated; they are harder to isolate, and even more difficult to implicate in the aetiology of a mental illness. The methods of psychiatric genetics are reasonably precise and unambiguous compared to the nature of the evidence which will be required to make a case for the operation of specific environmental factors; these have in many cases to be inferred from evidence gathered retrospectively or from unreliable sources, and do not always lend themselves to quantification and even semi-objective measurement. Those who stress that the origins of schizophrenia should be sought in particular patterns of family relationships and communication are hard pressed to provide evidence in other than anecdotal terms or at best to present a handful of cases selected on the basis of doubtful criteria.

As a matter of fact, few psychiatrists are now inclined to adopt extreme positions on this isuue. As scientists, they recognize the evidence for genetic factors derived from twin studies and related sources, while in the complementary role of clinician, they realize that many actual patients whom they encounter in the course of their work are largely the products of pathological social and environmental factors. In other words, whatever the scientific evidence may say about the likely extent of the genetic contribution to a disease in general, the psychiatrist still has to consider what kind of environmental factors might be operating in each individual case. At a clinical level, one finds many individuals in whom the probable contribution of genetic and environmental factors may depart substantially from the estimates for a whole population.

Twin studies of schizophrenia

The use of the twin method in studies of schizophrenia illustrates both the assets and the deficiencies of other twin studies in psychiatry. Research on this group of illnesses will now be considered in some detail; that on other mental disorders will be more briefly reviewed later. We shall take the work of Kallmann (1946, 1953) as a starting point because it was largely his findings which stimulated much later research, and also because his work illustrates some of the difficulties of psychiatric genetics which later investigators have tried to overcome.

In common with most other investigators, Kallmann used the concordance method. This involves searching the population of mental hospitals for twins with clearly established schizophrenia, and then making a careful study of the co-twin or of other family members to determine whether they too were schizophrenic. This method is obviously open to serious criticism, but before considering these, it will be as well to look at Kallmann's findings.

His original study (1946) included nearly 1000 schizophrenic patients (the so-called *index* cases) who had a twin and who were found by him from the records of all New York state hospitals from 1936 to 1946. Nearly 800 index cases whose co-twins survived past the age of fifteen were studied, of whom 174 pairs were MZ and 517 DZ. (In 103 pairs, both twins were index cases.) The raw data is reproduced in Table 21.

These figures have obviously to be corrected for age. Clearly, if the co-twin is still at risk for the development of schizophrenia, his age has to be taken into account, since this could distort the figures by underestimating genetic factors, Kallmann's explanation of the methods used to allow for age are far from clear, but he concluded that the concordance rates for MZ pairs should be raised to 85·8 per cent and those for DZ pairs to 14·7 per cent once an age correction had been applied. Similar problems were encountered by Slater (1953) who suggested that it would be

Table 21

Number of Twin Pairs Concordant for Schizophrenia (uncorrected data)

	MZ	DZ
Concordant	120	53
Discordant	54	464
Per cent concordance	69·0	10·3

Source: Kallmann (1946)

more realistic to study observed differences in age of onset in the concordant pairs. However, there is insufficient data in Kallmann's work to enable this to be done after the fact, or by others.

In addition to evidence from co-twins, Kallmann (1953) has also reported concordance data for other relatives. These are summarized in Table 22.

How far does data of this kind support a genetic interpretation, and, in so far as it does, does the evidence necessarily rule out the possibility of environmental determination? In the first place, it is abundantly clear that the risk of schizophrenia appears to increase regularly with increasing genetic relationship, with MZ twins showing a very high concordance, DZ pairs and siblings showing smaller but equal concordances, and half sibs and nephews and nieces showing systematically lower figures.

It has been argued, however, that such evidence does not necessarily provide evidence against an environmental aetiology, since 'the closer the blood relationship the more do the relatives also share the same traditions and live in the same milieu' (Davis, 1966, p. 52). That environmental factors play some part is suggested by the differences between separated and unseparated MZ pairs; on the other hand, one would expect on this argument that DZ twins would show substantially higher concordance rates than

Table 22

Concordance Rates for Families of Schizophrenics
(corrected for age)

	Per cent
MZ twins (not separated)	91·5
MZ twins (separated for five+ years)	77·6
MZ twins (total)	86·2
Two schizophrenic parents	68·1
One schizophrenic parent	16·4
DZ twins	14·5
Full sibs	14·2
Parents	9·2
Half sibs	7·1
Grandchildren	4·3
Nephews and nieces	3·9
First cousins	1·8
General population	0·9

Source: Kallmann (1953)

siblings, since the environment is more likely to have common characteristics for two children of the same age brought up in the same family. Similarly, it is of interest that half sibs should show exactly half the concordance rates of full sibs.

Before going further into the legitimacy of twin studies in psychiatry, it would be as well to summarize a number of other studies similar to Kallmann's. It will be apparent that

most of these find substantially higher M Z and D Z concordance in respect of schizophrenia. The single exception is
a Finnish study by Tienari (1963) who did not find a single
concordant M Z pair in a series of sixteen schizophrenic
twins. However, when these twins were followed up some
years later, M Z concordance was estimated to be 31 per
cent. The data are adapted from review papers by Shields,
Gottesman and Slater (1967) and Gottesman and Shields
(1966). Two more recent studies have been added, one by
Fischer, Harvald and Hauge (1969) from Denmark, and
another by Pollin (1969) and a large team of investigators
from the National Institute for Mental Health, Bethesda,
who drew on probably the largest population sample ever
studied. They obtained their data from a sample of 15,909
same-sexed 'veteran' twins, 'representing all the pairs of
white, male twins born in the decade 1917–27 and identified
as pairs, with both men serving in the Armed Forces during
the years spanning the Second World War and the Korean
War'. This study is also notable for its comparison of concordance rates for schizophrenia with those of a large
number of other diagnostic categories, ranging from neurosis to fractures.

These studies can leave little doubt about the facts, though
there is considerable room for doubt about their interpretation. In nearly all the studies, the M Z concordance is substantially higher than that found in D Z pairs, though the
actual proportions obviously vary considerably between
studies.

It now remains to consider some of the main objections
which have been levelled against the use of the twin method
in schizophrenia. Unfortunately, this has become a somewhat specialized research area, and the complexities of the
argument are not always easy to follow. For a comprehensive review, reference should be made to a recent monograph edited by Rosenthal and Kety entitled *The Transmission of Schizophrenia* (1968) which provides detailed
treatment of topics relating both to genetic and environmental factors which might be implicated in the develop-

Table 23

Concordance Rates of Twin Studies of Schizophrenia (uncorrected rates)

		MZ	%	DZ	%	*H*
Kallmann, 1946 (adults)	USA	120/174	69	34/296	11	0·65
Kallmann, 1956 (children)	USA	15/17	88	8/35	23	0·84
Slater, 1953	UK					
Resident sample		17/26	65	4/35	11	0·61
Consecutive sample		7/11	64	4/25	16	0·57
Essen-Moller, 1941	Sweden	7/11	64	4/27	15	0·58
Rosanoff *et al.*, 1934	USA	25/41	61	7/53	13	0·55
Inouye, 1961	Japan	33/55	60	2/11	18	0·51
Luxenburger, 1928	Germany	11/19	58	0/13	0	0·58
Gottesman and Shields, 1966	UK	10/24	42	3/33	9	0·36
Kringlen, 1964	Norway	2/8	25	2/12	17	0·10
Tienari, 1968	Finland	5/16	31	1/21	5	0·27
Fischer, Harvald and Hauge, 1969	Denmark	5/21	24	4/41	10	0·16
Pollin *et al.*, 1969	USA	11/80	14	6/146	4	0·10
All studies		268/503	53	79/748	11	0·47

Source: Shields, Gottesman and Slater (1967)

ment of schizophrenia. Particular attention is drawn to an important summary paper by Shields (1968), a review of earlier studies by Slater (1968), and a brave attempt at summary by Rosenthal (1968).

Definitions of schizophrenia

Perhaps the most fundamental difficulty is that of obtaining a concensus of agreement on the nature of schizophrenia. Psychiatrists do not always agree with each other in diagnosing schizophrenia even when they are colleagues in the same hospital and investigating the same patient (Ley, 1970). Furthermore, there are differences of emphasis between different clinics, and even more between different countries. British psychiatrists tend to believe that their American colleagues are inclined to diagnose schizophrenia rather more frequently than they do, and, in particular, that patients who in Britain might be regarded as suffering from severe anxiety states would be more likely to be regarded as schizophrenics in the USA. Again, further differences of emphasis are found in the Scandinavian countries where many of the important studies have been carried out. This problem cannot easily be resolved, partly because it is now commonly agreed that it may well be more appropriate to speak of 'the schizophrenias' rather than of a single discrete illness. There are elaborate classifications of schizophrenic illnesses which have advanced considerably beyond the previous divisions into simple, catatonic, hebephrenic and paranoid forms. Many investigators distinguish between 'process' schizophrenia which essentially takes a deteriorating course, though this may be quite prolonged, and all non-progressive forms, sometimes known under the name of 'reactive' schizophrenia. Psychological and experimental studies tend to favour a distinction between paranoid schizophrenics and other process manifestations (for examples see Venables, 1966).

Slater (1968) defines schizophrenia as follows:

Schizophrenia is an illness affecting the mind and the personality of the patient in a way which is seldom completely resolved: after an attack of illness there is nearly always some degree of permanent change of personality, and if there are several attacks this change will become more and more marked. The change is one that de-individualizes and dehumanizes the patient, and leaves him, above all, with impaired capacities for normal and affective responses. While an attack of illness is proceeding there will be one or more of a series of distinctive symptoms: hallucinations in a clear state of consciousness, passivity-feelings, primary delusional experiences, and rather typical forms of thought disorder (p. 15).

In the same volume, however, Bleuler (1968) who can also claim a lifetime's clinical and research experience with schizophrenic patients and their families, offers a definition with a more favourable prognosis:

> More than twenty or thirty years after the onset of a severe schizophrenic psychosis, the general tendencies are towards an improvement. . . . It is true that it is mostly a partial improvement, but it consists of a real reappearance of both healthy intellectual life and a very warm-hearted, very emotional life in certain situations and in contact with certain persons (p. 6).

We need not be unduly discouraged by these contrasting definitions. Despite differences of emphasis, it appears that the frequency with which schizophrenia is recorded shows

Table 24

Expectation of Schizophrenia for the General Population

Date	Country	Expectation %	Standard error
1931	Switzerland	1·23	0·368
1936	Germany	0·51	0·088
1942	Denmark	0·69	0·054
1942	Finland	0·91	0·021
1946	Sweden	0·81	0·087
1959	Japan	0·82	0·088
1964	Iceland	0·73	0·121

Source: Slater (1968)

quite a considerable degree of agreement in a variety of environments over the world. It seems that schizophrenia occurs in most countries with about the same frequency, and that variations in frequency are to some extent attributable to artefacts such as systems of recording, the adequacy of hospital services and similar factors. This may be illustrated by a table of Slater's (1968) summarizing the expectation of schizophrenia for the general population in a number of different societies.

Slater argues that the fair measure of agreement in the frequency of schizophrenia constitutes an argument in favour of a strong genetic element; his argument is presumably based on the fact that considerable social and environmental variations between different societies nevertheless result in roughly similar expectations of schizophrenia. Be that as it may, we still have to note that the incidence of schizophrenia has so far been adequately studied in relatively few countries, and that more representative surveys may well yield greater variance.

Moreover the incidence of schizophrenia within each society is substantially greater in working class than in middle class environments. This at least was the conclusion of an exhaustive review of the subject by Kohn (1968): amongst numerous studies he cites an important British study by Goldberg and Morrison (1963) who reported that while male schizophrenics admitted to hospital showed the usual proportions of patients from the lowest social classes, their fathers' occupations were more normally distributed. To some extent this study supports the 'downward social drift' hypothesis, but it has also been argued that working class membership is in itself sufficiently stressful to act as a precipitant to psychosis (see also Goldberg, 1968).

Contamination of diagnosis

Criticism has also been directed against the danger of contaminated diagnosis specific to a twin study. The investigator with a genetic bias is, on this argument, more likely to make a diagnosis of schizophrenia or indeed of any psychiatric disorder in the co-twin of a known schizophrenic than if he were to encounter the same individual in the course of a routine psychiatric examination. This criticism has been most frequently levelled against Kallmann's studies. A similar criticism would imply that his knowledge of the zygosity of the twin pair might have influenced his diagnosis of the co-twin: in other words, he might have shown unconscious bias towards making identical diagnoses by knowing that he was dealing with an identical pair of twins. It has also been suggested that his judgement of zygosity, at least in doubtful cases, might have been similarly influenced by his knowledge of the diagnosis.

Kallmann's data has recently been re-evaluated in the light of these criticisms by Shields, Gottesman and Slater (1967). They agree that he laid himself open to criticism by failing to specify certain critical variables: for example, how many of the co-twins whom he called schizophrenic were actually hospitalized, and for how many was the diagnosis changed by him? The relevant information on these points is summarized by them in Table 25.

Examination of the right hand column of the table indicates that of 173 'second twins' (both M Z and D Z) 73·4 per cent had also been diagnosed as schizophrenic by mental hospital staff, 81·5 per cent had been patients in a mental hospital, and 86·7 were regarded by Kallmann as definite cases of schizophrenia. Only fourteen cases had their diagnoses changed to schizophrenia as a result of Kallmann's examination. From their study of this previously unpublished material, Shields, Gottesman and Slater (1967) conclude: 'From this information and despite the absence of representative case histories, we do not believe that Kallmann was too free in labelling co-twins as schizophrenic' (p. 388). They also showed that 94 per cent of Kallmann's definite schizophrenics had been in a mental hospital, and that he diagnosed as definitely or questionably schizophrenic only one co-twin who had never been in hospital for every 4·41 so admitted (32 : 141).

With regard to the criticism that his knowledge of zygosity influenced the diagnosis, Shields, Gottesman and Slater (1967) show that there is a complete lack of evidential support for the notion that Kallmann may have allowed knowledge of the independent variable (zygosity) to influence his judgement of the dependent variable (diagnosis) in the direction of calling doubtful pairs concordant because he knew

Table 25

Cumulative Pairwise Concordance (uncorrected for age) of Kallmann's Twin Study (1946) as a Function of Various Criteria

Second twin	MZ		DZ		Total schizophrenic second twins
	N	%	*N*	%	*N*
Had mental hospital diagnosis of schizophrenia on first investigation	87/174	50·0	31/517	6·0	118
or: By end of study	95/174	54·6	32/517	6·2	127
or: In mental hospital diagnosed by Kallmann as schizophrenic	100/174	57·5	41/517	7·9	141
or: Diagnosed by Kallmann as definite schizophrenia	103/174	59·2	47/517	9·1	150
or: Diagnosed by Kallmann as schizophrenia, inclusive of suspected schizophrenia	120/174	69·0	53/517	10·3	173

Source: Shields, Gottesman and Slater (1967)

them to be M Z (p. 390). They show that the relative increase in M Z concordance resulting from the inclusion of a co-twin who did not have a hospital diagnosis of schizophrenia was in fact much smaller (26·3 per cent) than the increase in D Z concordance (65·6 per cent). This table is not reproduced here.

These matters have been discussed in considerable detail

mainly because Kallmann's work is frequently subjected to severe criticism in textbooks and elsewhere, and tends to be summarily dismissed as speculative, badly conducted and even as quite worthless. Although it is true that Kallmann was at fault in failing to provide enough detail in his publications, the re-analysis of his original material by the Maudsley group has shown with considerable force that the criticisms are largely unjustified. It seems necessary, therefore, to rehabilitate Kallmann's work into the important position it deserves in the literature on this subject – a literature which partly substantiates his original conclusions. Nevertheless, later studies, as summarized in Table 23, mostly report lower absolute concordance figures for MZ twins, even though these are in most cases still higher than for DZ pairs.

This discrepancy between Kallmann's figures of MZ concordance and those of later workers may be at least in part related to differences in severity. Cases studied in recent years have usually been less severely affected than Kallmann's index cases. Advances in chemotherapy, particularly the introduction of the chlorpromazine and phenothiazine group of drugs since the mid-1950s, may have contributed to lower incidence or to reduced severity in the symptomatology. More schizophrenic illnesses are being treated at an early stage, and on an out-patient basis; moreover, the clinical picture of a 'true' schizophrenia might be somewhat obscured by the use of drug therapy; Kallmann's studies, both in Germany before the War, and subsequently in the USA during the period 1936–46, were virtually conducted in a different psychiatric era, with the result that his schizophrenics may have shown more obvious or more florid symptoms. This provides a rather telling example of one way in which a condition with a substantial genetic component comes to be modified in its expression by an important environmental factor which previously played a less critical part. A similar example is phenylketonuria, which can now be partly treated by environmental intervention given in the form of a special diet.

Other objections to the twin method

It has been suggested that MZ twins may be especially vulnerable to schizophrenic illness because of their special relationship to each other, which might involve confusions of identity and weak ego development. Moreover, it might be argued that the very existence of a close relationship between the twins might isolate them from the mother and the rest of society. As Shields (1968) points out, such an argument would lead one to expect that schizophrenia would be commoner in MZ than in DZ twins, but this is not the case, nor is schizophrenia commoner in twins than in the population as a whole. It has also been suggested that concordance rates might be spuriously raised by the identification between MZ twins; in other words, a potentially normal twin might become psychotic as a result of his close identification with his affected twin. On the other hand, the process might work equally the other way, so that a potential schizophrenic might be prevented from falling ill by virtue of identification with his normal twin. Little evidence exists to support or refute these suggestions; nevertheless, it is surprising that very few cases of *folie à deux* are found in twins.

Thirdly, there exists a possibility that MZ twins are more at risk because they might be equally exposed to an adverse environment such as would be provided by a pathogenic parent. Here again, evidence is hard to come by, but Kallmann (1946) did report higher concordance in pairs brought up together than in those that had been separated for more than five years.

These objections cannot be answered directly from the twin studies themselves. If they were valid, however, we would expect to find other evidence of environmental bias serious enough to cast doubt on the validity of twin studies. Arguments for the strength of environmental factors come not from twin studies but from studies of families of schizophrenic patients. Such studies are beyond the scope of this book, but they are well represented in the Puerto Rico proceedings in contributions by Wynne (1968) and Lidz (1968) who lay particular stress on patterns of family interaction which have been held to contribute to psychotic illness. We must therefore try to summarize some of the environmental variables which have been implicated in the genesis of schizophrenia.

Before doing so, however, it must be stressed that virtually none of the participants at the conference was prepared to claim that schizophrenia could be explained purely and simply in terms of either genetic or environmental variables. Disagreements seemed to be expressed more in terms of shades of emphasis than in hard dichotomies. In other words, it was agreed that genetic and environmental factors must be viewed as interacting in a complex and subtle way. Even the more extreme protagonists of an environmental and familial view were prepared to admit the strength of the genetic evidence: as already pointed out, the geneticists have an advantage over their opponents, since the nature of the evidence which they produce from twin studies and from other sources is inevitably much more precise and specific because quantitative measures can be used, which can be repeated and tested for reliability and validity. The environmentalists, on the other, are handicapped by the need to use more impressionistic and intuitive sources of evidence (see also Laing and Esterson, 1964).

Two types of environmental factor have been suggested as possibly relevant in the aetiology of schizophrenia: biological and social (Rosenthal, 1968).

Biological. It is now generally accepted that environmental variables are not purely social and cultural, but also have biological effects, and that these can be thought of as beginning to operate from the moment of conception, when the zygote and later the embryo and foetus develop in a complex biological environment. It is becoming increasingly clear that differences between MZ pairs, including discordance for schizophrenia, might be related to biological differences, even if we have only crude indices of such differences. Pollin and Stabenau (1968) reported that the healthy twin in discordant MZ pairs is in many cases the heavier of the two at birth, that the schizophrenic twin shows more 'soft' neurological signs, has more episodes of disturbed sleep and restlessness as an infant, and also shows certain bio-chemical disturbances, including lower protein bound iodine levels and higher lactate/pyruvate ratios. However, they also found that the weaker twin tended to be overprotected, and showed a marked dependency not only on his mother, but also on his co-twin. Their study therefore leaves open the question of the priority of biological or social factors in the origins of schizophrenia.

Pollin's study is unique in concentrating on discordant MZ pairs. As a result, the findings have not been widely confirmed by other workers, though there do appear to be fairly definite indications of a relationship between higher birth weight and discordance (e.g. the case study reported by McSweeney, 1970). Similar findings have been reported for intelligence and for behavioural characteristics in at least two other recent studies. The first is a study by Willerman and Churchill (1967) who found, for two different groups of identical twins aged between five and fifteen, that the twin with the lower birth weight also had the lower verbal and performance IQs on the Wechsler Intelligence Scale for Children; the trend was particularly marked for performance tests. Secondly, Brown, Stafford and Vandenberg (1967) reported that the twin with the lower birth weight was said by his mother to smile more, and to be more like his mother, but to have a greater number of problems with feeding and sleeping. However, many other behaviours did not show significant differences either between heavier and lighter, or between first- and second-born twins. Again, we seem to be confronted with an interaction between biological and social factors: the weaker twin tends to elicit more protective behaviour from the mother, who therefore seems to be providing a slightly different 'micro-environment' for him. Experience of interviewing mothers of young twins certainly suggests that they are aware of and responsive to the slightest differences between them, and respond very articulately to any invitation to describe these differences.

Social. Genetic and environmental factors are nowhere more confusingly confounded than in trying to interpret the family interactions of schizophrenic parents. If we know that the patient's mother was herself a diagnosed schizophrenic, what kind of evidence would be needed to show that the patient's schizophrenia was genetically transmitted by his mother, or environmentally determined as a result of the disordered or at least atypical environment created by a schizophrenic mother for her children? In others words, can schizophrenic symptoms and behaviour be learned by identification or modelling? Similarly, could certain child-rearing patterns or intermittent bizarre and unusual behaviour in the mother finally result in her child's schizophrenia? Or is it possible that a patient with incipient psychosis could himself be the cause of psychotic reactions in the family?

These are highly complex issues, to which no satisfactory answer has been found. The case for familial factors was argued in considerable detail by several participants to the Puerto Rico conference, but it is notable that none of them claimed that such factors could produce schizophrenia in the absence of genetic or constitutional disposition. Nevertheless, they were justified in accusing genetic investigators of too easily disregarding environmental factors. The difficulty facing environmentalists is partly one of specifying their variables with sufficient precision to make them amenable to research. Lidz (1968) confined himself to intensive observations, with special reference to disturbances of communication in schizophrenic families (including the so-called 'double-bind' hypothesis), while Wynne (1968) discussed 'ways in which the family destroys the child's efforts to maintain a focus of attention'. Summarizing these studies, McMahon (1968) points out that the issue is not so much whether environmental factors are *involved*, but whether they can be *identified*. We might go further and require them to be identified by reliable and repeatable methods. So far the verdict with respect to the role of the family in the genesis of schizophrenia must remain 'not proven'.

Nevertheless, the matter need not be entirely left there. On the assumption that environmental factors are indeed important, even if not fully quantifiable, we can at least look for indirect evidence of their operation. For example, we can examine children who are placed for adoption as babies because their mothers are suffering from schizophrenia. If such children develop normally, or at least show a lower frequency for the disease, then it might be assumed that a favourable environment has 'prevented' the condition.

Such evidence is now becoming available from a number of studies. There is a study by Heston (1966, 1968) who compared forty-seven adoptees separated from their schizophrenic mothers at birth with fifty controls born to non-schizophrenic mothers: about half of each group were reared in foundling homes and the other half in adoptive families. All the subjects were followed up at thirty-five years, and compared on a number of ratings of psychiatric disability. The results are summarized in Table 26.

This table reflects a number of interesting findings. On an overall rating of mental health (Menninger Mental Health Sickness Rating Scale) the experimental group (i.e. children of schizophrenic mothers) had significantly poorer ratings (i.e. lower scores). All psychiatric disorders including schizophrenia were significantly commoner in the experimental group compared to the controls. The percentage of schizophrenic children where one parent was schizophrenic was 16·6 – the identical percentage reported by Kallmann (1946), using age-corrected figures. Although these findings provide strong support for a genetic hypothesis, Heston reports other material which is of even greater interest. The experimental group, despite being psychiatrically vulnerable and disabled, nevertheless contained a higher proportion of somewhat artistic individuals than the controls. Seven showed unusual musical ability, six were deeply religious;

Table 26

Comparison of Adoptees of Schizophrenic and
Normal Mothers

	Control ($N = 50$)	Experimental ($N = 47$)	Exact probability
Age, mean	36·3	35·8	
Adopted	19	22	
Mental health ratings	80·1	65·2	0·001
Schizophrenia	0	5	0·024
Mental deficiency	0	4	0·052
Sociopathic	2	9	0·017
Neurotic disorder	7	13	0·052
More than one year in penal or psychiatric institution	2	11	0·006
Total years institution	15	112	0·001
Felons	2	7	0·054
Number serving in armed forces	17	21	
Discharged from forces	1	8	0·021
Mean I Q	103·7	94·0	
Years in school	12·4	11·6	
Number of children	84	71	
Divorces	7	6	
Social group, first home	4·2	4·5	
Social group, second home	4·7	5·4	

Source: Heston and Denny (1968)

however, alcoholism was also commoner. These findings
suggest that whatever the genetic mechanisms involved, they
are not necessarily specific to schizophrenia; genes which
lead to schizophrenia in one set of circumstances may be
associated with artistic achievements in another.

Findings complementary to Heston's have also been reported by an American–Danish research group (Kety *et al.*,
1968; Rosenthal *et al.*, 1968). Every attempt was made in

these studies to exclude all sources of bias or contamination, and a large number of investigators was involved. They compared the incidence of schizophrenic disorders in adoptees whose biological parents had a history of schizophrenia with a control group of adoptees without such a history. Of 150 biological relatives of index cases (i.e. adoptees with schizophrenia) 8·7 per cent also had a history of schizophrenia, compared to 1·9 per cent of the controls ($p = 0.007$).

Other mental disorders

The preceding review of twin studies in psychiatry has concentrated on schizophrenic disorders because these have been investigated with the greatest thoroughness, and also because they best illustrate the advantages and disadvantages of the twin methed in psychiatry. But other mental disorders have also been studied by genetic techniques, and these will now be more briefly reviewed.

Manic-depressive psychoses

These are essentially disorders of mood or affect, with a tendency to remission and recurrence. It is common to distinguish between neurotic (reactive) and psychotic (endogenous) depressions, though this distinction is not universally accepted. Depressive illnesses are much commoner than the manic variety, though some patients show severe mood swings from elation to depression. Other symptoms found in association with psychotic depression include mental and motor 'retardation' (i.e. slowness and lethargy), perplexity, agitation and delusions. Unlike schizophrenia, manic-depressive illnesses are essentially diseases of middle-age. They should however be distinguished from the senile or involutional melancholias (Wittenborn, 1965).

The main twin investigations have again been conducted by Kallmann (1953), who reported a concordance rate of 96 per cent in identical twins, and 26 per cent in fraternals. These figures should be compared against a baseline incidence in the general population of 0·4 per cent, and concordance rates of 23 per cent both in parents and sibs, and 17 per cent in half-sibs. These differences are consistent with the operation of genetic mechanisms. Similar findings were reported by Luxenburger (1942) (MZ 91 per cent, DZ 6 per cent) and Rosanoff, Handy and Plesset (1935) (MZ 70 per cent, DZ 16 per cent). For involutional psychosis, Kallmann reported concordance rates of 60 per cent for MZ and 6 per cent for DZ pairs, again compared with 6 per cent for both parents and siblings. Comparable figures for the wider category of senile psychoses were 43 per cent and 8 per cent in MZ and DZ pairs respectively. Although these figures are strongly suggestive of genetic factors in depressive illnesses, the studies have not been as thoroughly conducted or as systematically checked as the parallel studies in schizophrenia.

Homosexuality

At first sight, Kallmann's (1952) remarkably high 100 per cent MZ concordance rate compared to 11 per cent in the DZ sample might be dismissed as an environmental artefact, were it not that most of the twins claim to have developed their homosexual interests independently of each other, and also denied any significant history of mutual sex relations. Even if these denials were untrue, it would still be necessary to explain another finding from the same study, which indicated an unexpectedly large number of male siblings in the sibships of male homosexual twins, and also in sibships of other male homosexuals. Kallmann found a ratio of 126 males to 100 females, as compared with the expected ratio of 106 to 100. A German study by Lang (1940) reported similarly unusual ratios in a large study of over 1000 male homosexuals. These findings have been interpreted by Hurst (1965) as evidence for homosexuality as a biologically determined phenomenon on a genetic basis, i.e. as 'due to a genetically disarranged balance between male and female maturational tendencies' (Hurst, 1965, p. 164). Nevertheless, environmental and psychodynamic factors are undoubtedly important (see also Slater, 1962; Bene, 1965; Heston and Shields, 1968).

Neurotic and character disorders

The precise diagnosis of neurotic and behaviour disorders presents obvious difficulties, but a number of twin and other studies of family resemblances have been reported in the literature. As usual, identical twins show higher concordance rates than fraternal twins on a number of indices of behaviour disorder, delinquency and crime. Some of these studies are summarized in Table 27.

Table 27

Concordance Rates for Identical and Fraternal Twins for Neurotic and Character Disorders

	MZ		DZ	
	N	% concordance	N	% concordance
Adult crime	107	71	118	34
Juvenile delinquency	42	85	25	75
Childhood behaviour disorder	47	87	60	43
Alcoholism	26	65	56	30

Source: Eysenck (1964)

A review by Stabenau, Pollin and Allen (1970) of data from ten studies of neurosis is summarized in Table 28. The largest of these is the NIMH study by Pollin *et al.* (1969) who reported data from 996 pairs of neurotic male twins who were USA army veterans. Concordance rates were 9 per cent for MZ and 7 per cent for DZ twins. In this study the concordance ratios (MZ/DZ) for neurosis were no higher than those for fractures. Summing all ten studies of neurosis, the MZ/DZ concordance ratio is substantially lower than those for schizophrenia.

Table 28

Pairwise Concordance Rates (uncorrected for age)
for Ten Studies of Neurosis

| | MZ *pairs* | | DZ *pairs* | | MZ/DZ |
| | % | | % | | *concordance* |
	N	*concordance*	N	*concordance*	*ratio*
Stumpfl (1937)	7	43	9	0	
Slater (1953)	8	25	40	13	2·0
Shields (1954)	23	74	18	50	1·5
Slater (1961)	12	42	12	33	1·3
Ihda (1961)	20	50	5	40	1·3
Braconi (1961)	20	90	30	43	2·1
Tienari (1963)	21	57			
Inouye (1965)	21	48	5	40	1·2
Parker (1966)	9	67	11	36	1·8
Pollin *et al.* (1969)	419	9	577	7	1·3

Source: Pollin *et al.* (1969)

In another study, Slater and Shields (cited by Eysenck, 1967) have shown that the difference in concordance between MZ and DZ twins increases as the diagnostic criteria are made more specific. Their results are shown in Table 29.

Shields (1954) has also shown that the degree of closeness in the relationship between identical pairs did not affect concordance figures.

A detailed study of obsessional neurosis in a pair of twins has recently been published by Marks *et al.* (1969) who also review earlier reports of high concordance for this condition. In their study, however, the treated twin failed to respond to desensitization therapy, and did not improve as a result of separation from his even more severely affected and dominant co-twin.

Table 29

Concordance in Psychiatric Diagnosis in M Z and D Z Twins in Relation to Specificity of Diagnosis (International Classification of Diseases)

	MZ (N = 80)	DZ (N = 112)	MZ/DZ ratio
Any coded abnormality in co-twin	50·0	29·5	1·7
Both twins neurosis or personality disorder or both psychiatric disorder	37·5	14·3	2·6
Both twins psychotic, neurotic or personality disorder	31·3	8·9	3·5
Both twins same diagnostic code (whole number)	28·8	3·6	8·1
Both twins same diagnostic code (smallest subdivision)	25·0	2·7	9·3

Source: Eysenck (1967a)

Mental subnormality

Twin studies in the sphere of severe mental subnormality must obviously be distinguished from studies examining genetic factors in normal intellectual functioning, and are therefore usually restricted to the use of the concordance method to compare twins who have a demonstrable mental defect. In other words, it is more convenient to study severely subnormal rather than mildly subnormal (or educationally subnormal) twins, because in the latter group it is difficult to separate genetic from environmental factors.

But difficulties arise even if investigation of twins is limited to those with severe subnormality because twins are more vulnerable to the effects of early damage to the brain and central nervous system than singletons. In general, subnormal twins are found in greater than expected proportions both in hospitals for the mentally subnormal and in the community (Berg and Kirman, 1960). Moreover, differences even within an identical pair may not be due either to heredity or environment in the normal sense of these terms, but rather to the different exposure of one twin to the obstetric and other biological hazards inherent in twinning. Thus, the second born twin may suffer from anoxia or brain damage due to pre-natal or peri-natal difficulties (see chapter 4). There is, furthermore, evidence from case studies that one identical twin may be severely subnormal and the other normal (Hinden, 1956; Brandon, Kirman and Williams, 1959).

Surveys of large populations of mentally subnormal people conducted in the Scandinavian countries, have generally reported significantly higher concordance figures for identical than for fraternal pairs. These studies are summarized by Böök (1953) and Shields and Slater (1960); combining figures from two early studies of over 550 pairs yields a concordance rate of 96 per cent for MZ and 56 per cent for DZ pairs.

In general, evidence for the contribution of hereditary factors to mental subnormality is derived not so much from twin studies but from an examination of family pedigrees (Reed and Reed, 1965) and from more detailed biochemical and other clinical investigations. These studies now tend to be concerned with the genetics of specific syndromes rather than with mental handicap as a whole (Penrose, 1963; Berg, 1965).

Conclusions

It will be obvious that no one is nowadays inclined to seek the origins of mental disorders either in genetics or environment alone. To speak in terms of an interaction between them is to do no more than state the obvious, and yet we understand very little of the mechanisms which might underlie such an interaction. Research studies already available have provided useful data both on the genetic and environmental side, but interpretation of the data is limited by the relative crudity of the information available. In other words, we can be fairly certain from the evidence that both genetic and environmental factors play a substantial role in the development of, for example, schizophrenia, but present knowledge does not extend to any particularly penetrating insights into the nature of the actual genetic mechanisms involved, or the kind of environmental processes that seem to make people particularly vulnerable to psychotic illnesses.

Evidence for the importance of genetic factors has been collected from different types of study, of which twin studies are only one example. We have seen that most of the twin studies show substantially higher MZ than DZ concordance. We have looked at some of the criticisms levelled against the twin method and conclude that these do not on the whole invalidate either the method or the findings. In addition to twin studies, at least two other types of evidence have been considered: the first is derived from consanguinity studies, which have shown that the risk of schizophrenia rises in direct proportion to the closeness of the genetic relationship with an affected relative. The second line of evidence comes from an examination of the surprisingly small variations in the incidence of schizophrenia in different societies. Finally, recent studies of adopted children who were separated from their schizophrenic mothers at birth indicate that the risk of schizophrenia in such children is as great as if they had been brought up by one schizophrenic parent, and much greater than that of a control group of adoptees whose natural mothers were not schizophrenic.

Despite the strong trend of the evidence, it is clear that geneticists have made little headway in identifying the nature of the genetic mechanisms involved. Various models have been proposed, the main candidates being a simple Mendelian mode of transmission, a single dominant gene and a recessive type of inheritance; the more widely favoured model is a polygenic model involving many genes, not unlike the model that has been suggested for the inheritance of intellectual abilities. Various authorities have claimed to find evidence for each of these theories but none is generally accepted.

More relevant to psychologists, however, is the nature of the environmental processes that might be involved in producing schizophrenia. If this condition is the result of an interaction between genetic and environmental factors, it is obviously important to try and pin down the nature of the environmental determinants, so that preventive measures can be taken wherever possible. Unfortunately, the lack of detailed information again makes it difficult to advance beyond rather vague generalizations. The variables isolated by research are often non-specific, and refer to constructs that have so far defied more precise analysis.

Social class provides a convenient example. It is clear that schizophrenia occurs more commonly in working-class than in middle-class patients, though many of the patients who become schizophrenics have shown 'downward social drift' from an originally higher social class position: however, it has also been suggested that working class membership *per se* constitutes one form of stressful environmental precipitant. At the level of family interaction studies, we have a number of speculative hypotheses involving faulty patterns of communication within the family, and particularly from the mother to the patient, but these are by their very nature difficult to establish by the criteria of objective research. In this respect, therefore, investigators who wish to identify and isolate environmental variables are at a disadvantage compared to their colleagues who choose to work within a biological framework.

The study of twins discordant for schizophrenia provides one example of this difficulty. Biologically oriented research workers have shown that the healthy twin has other biological advantages compared to his more handicapped co-twin. He tends to be heavier at birth, and to show relatively fewer signs of difficulty in his early development: moreover, his biochemical constitution seems to be somewhat sounder from the start. Unfortunately, we have almost no information on the social and personality development of discordant twin pairs, and no developmental case studies of separated identical twins discordant for schizophrenia. Admittedly, these would be very hard to find.

Perhaps we can conclude that what is inherited is not schizophrenia, but a predisposition to schizophrenia. Whether or not the individual will actually become schizophrenic depends on a complex of factors, which have not been satisfactorily identified. We know, however, that even when both parents are affected, the chances of their offspring developing the illness are not more than two in three. This may be due to partial penetrance of the genes involved, but on the other hand it may be largely attributable to the cushioning effects of a favourable set of environmental circumstances. The nature of these circumstances has yet to be discovered, but when it is, we shall have at our disposal a therapeutic weapon at least as powerful as drugs.

Part Three **Overview**

8 Conclusions

The aim of this book has been to reinstate twin studies to their proper place in psychology. They are not, as many people imagine, merely the product of an outmoded, oversimplified and sterile controversy, but have made a considerable contribution to a number of important contemporary issues in the developmental sciences, among which psychology is only one. Indeed, far from being outmoded, twin studies are likely to play an even more important part in the future; this is largely because we are only just beginning to ask more searching questions.

One of the reasons why the nature-nurture controversy proved relatively unproductive in the 1930s was that the questions and terminology were too global. We are now beginning to see that terms such as 'heredity', 'environment', 'intelligence', 'personality' are themselves of limited value in research, even though they provide convenient abbreviations with a common core of meaning for general discussion. Psychologists are becoming increasingly dissatisfied with global constructs such as 'intelligence', 'language', 'perception', 'memory' and 'learning'; recent theoretical and psychometric efforts have concentrated on attempts to isolate, identify and measure specific cognitive processes. General intelligence has never been satisfactorily defined, even though theoretically adequate and empirically useful assessment instruments have been developed. Intelligence is now seen as consisting of a number of hierarchically organized skills and processes; these are far from easy to isolate, since a substantial proportion of the variance is still accounted for by a general factor, but research on the new British Intelligence Scale has suggested that a multifactorial approach to the assessment of specific intellectual abilities is worth while (Warburton *et al.*, 1970). Similarly, some progress has been made in breaking down the global constructs of language and perception and trying to identify their underlying components (McCarthy and Kirk, 1961; Kirk, McCarthy and Kirk, 1968; Frostig, Lefever and Whittlesey, 1964). Learning is probably too complex to be analysed by psychometric methods alone; these will need to be supplemented by behaviouristic methods in which an individual's response to a specific learning situation will be objectively described (see Mittler, 1970a, 1970b for fuller discussions of these developments).

Attempts to measure specific abilities are of obvious relevance to twin studies, since we can at the very least use the classical twin study method to compare the performance of identical and fraternal pairs on tests of special abilities. We can then see whether some tests appear to be more strongly influenced by genetic factors than others, and even produce a rank order of the sub-tests in respect of the strength of their genetic contribution (Vandenberg, 1968; Mittler, 1969b). Such studies must be interpreted with caution, since the use of tests of specific abilities inevitably raises the question of their reliability; furthermore, low reliability also reduces the validity of comparisons between one sub-test and another. Nevertheless, the method appears promising, and certainly constitutes an advance on the use of global intelligence tests alone, even though these have given remarkably consistent results. For example, the ITPA twin study suggested that genetic factors were more important for the visual-motor than for the auditory-vocal channel, and independent evidence from studies of singleton children has confirmed that auditory-vocal tests are strongly influenced by environmental variables such as social class (Mittler and Ward, 1970).

Attempts to study specific cognitive abilities are paralleled by work on specific environmental components. Psychologists and sociologists have tended to talk in general and global terms about the effects of environment on language and intelligence, but it has never been very clear whether some aspects of the environment contribute more to these effects than others. Attempts are now being made to describe these processes in greater detail, and to use statistical methods (such as step-wise multiple regression) which express the relative importance of each of the many factors involved.

The Manchester surveys reported by Wiseman (1964, 1966, 1967) provide a convenient example, though other large scale studies have concerned themselves with these problems, and reached similar conclusions (Pringle, Butler and Davie, 1966; Fraser, 1959; Douglas, 1964, 1968). Wiseman studied a population of ten-year olds from forty-four primary schools; intelligence and attainment test results from the age of seven were available, together with ratings on a total of fifty-two environmental variables – eighteen concerned with home and neighbourhood, thirty-four with school buildings, equipment, teachers and 'atmosphere'. The findings indicated that younger children are relatively more affected by environmental variables than older ones, that the effects of adverse environments are greatest on the abler children, and that home and neighbourhood variables, particularly those concerned with the quality of care in the home, affect educational attainment even more than factors in the school.

Studies such as these indicate that environmental components can be identified objectively, if not comprehensively. Some are inevitably too complicated to lend themselves to quantification, but others can be unambiguously identified. Wiseman reported positive correlations between school performance and the following variables: cleanliness of the home, proportion of verminous children, inadequate provision for material needs, eligibility for free meals, parental occupation. Significant correlations were also reported with streaming, attendance and sociability. Other examples of the effect of specific environmental variables are amply documented in the Plowden Report (Central Advisory Council on Education, 1967).

In addition to the home and school variables already mentioned, attempts are being made to describe in detail the nature of the linguistic environment in which a child lives; the work of Bernstein (1965) has had a strong influence here, and some of his associates have been developing techniques to describe the nature of the language which mothers use, particularly in response to the child's questions (Robinson and Rackstraw, 1967). Despite these advances, much needs to be learned about the nature and mode of operation of environmental variables; social class is still the most widely used index of 'environment' and in its simplest form is, of course, an extremely global concept; it has however been shown to be of profound significance in many aspects of child-rearing (e.g. Newson and Newson, 1968); other variables may be as general as 'tender loving care', or as specific as the syntactic structures used by the mother. In other words, environmental variables range from the molar to the molecular.

To a certain extent, the same statement might be made of genetic variables. The term 'genetic' tends to be used more loosely by psychologists than by geneticists, just as the term 'environmental' is probably less precisely defined by geneticists than by psychologists. In the field of human behaviour, particularly in relation to continuously varying characteristics, such as height or intelligence, geneticists appear to be in agreement that in so far as genetic mechanisms are involved at all, the processes involve not one gene but many. A lucid summary is provided by Carter (1966).

It is very probable that the genetic component in the development of intelligence is polygenic, that it depends on many pairs of gene loci on many different chromosome pairs, and that there are multiple alleles, i.e. alternative forms of a gene, at most of these gene loci. A very simple model for the situation at one of these gene loci is that in which there are three alleles – the commonest with a frequency of, say, one-half, which tends to give average intelligence, say an IQ of 100; another with frequency of one quarter which tends to give a score ten points above average intelligence; the third also with frequency of one quarter which tends to give a score ten points below average in intelligence. If marriage is not assortative for intelligence, this would give a population distribution of intelligence ... in which one-sixteenth of the population is very bright or very dull, with scores of 120 or eighty respectively, one quarter being moderately bright or moderately dull, scoring 110 or ninety respectively, and half being at or around the average score of 100 (pp. 186–7).

Carter's model, admittedly oversimplified, rests on assumptions which are not tenable; for example, that assortative mating does not take place although we know that it does, as shown by average correlations of 0·5 between spouses' IQs; moreover, as he points out, the presence of more than one gene locus would increase the variance and smooth the distribution; the same result would be achieved by further environmental differences.

Geneticists seem less concerned with the extent of genetic as opposed to environmental contributions to human behaviour than with advancing our understanding of the actual genetic mechanisms involved. Fundamental advances have been made in unravelling the complex role of RNA and DNA in the transmission of genetic 'information', but other workers are developing biometrical methods of analysing twin data collected by psychologists. These methods, which are described in detail by Jinks and Fulker (1970), aim to incorporate both classical correlational studies and also Cattell's multivariate methods (MAVA) in an attempt to assess the kind of gene action and the kind of mating system operating in the population.

Twin studies now have fewer political overtones than in the 1930s, though these are not entirely absent, as the controversy following Jensen's (1969) paper has shown. Nevertheless, it may be useful to set twin studies against the broader background of the recent interest on the part of psychologists in biological aspects of behaviour.

In a major review, Vandenberg (1966) traces the renewal of interest in hereditary components of behaviour to certain key advances in the biological sciences. Perhaps the most significant are the 'breakthroughs' in the field of human genetics, of which the most striking examples were the discovery of an extra chromosome in Down's syndrome (mongolism), quickly followed by further discoveries of other chromosome abnormalities, particularly in the sex chromosomes. Even more fundamental developments can be expected from the advances in the understanding of basic genetic material which stem from the Watson–Crick discovery of the complex role of DNA and RNA.

One of the earliest examples of applied genetic research was the finding that a specific type of mental subnormality (Phenylketonuria, or PKU) was due to lack of an enzyme (phenylalanine hydroxylase) which is necessary to convert phenylalanine to tyrosine in normal digestion. Toxicity of developing brain cells results from unconverted phenylalanine. Vandenberg (1966) points out that the PKU discovery illustrates three important concepts in modern genetics. The first is the 'one gene–one enzyme' theory – 'the concept that a single gene determines the characteristics of one specific enzyme'. The second is that of 'carrier detection' – the concept that a 'carrier' can be identified by a phenylalanine tolerance test, and appropriate genetic counselling provided. The third concept is that of 'modifiability of the gene-environment complex', which means that the effects of a metabolic lesion can be reduced by an alteration in the environment. In the case of PKU it has been suggested (Woolf *et al.*, 1958), but by no means proved (Birch and Tizard, 1967), that a diet low in phenylalanine can reduce the degree of mental retardation in a high proportion of cases.

Another review by Meissner (1965) is also relevant in the context of fundamental developments in human genetics. Meissner draws attention to the distinction between 'structural' genes which control eye colour, height and PKU, and 'regulator' or 'operator' genes which serve to regulate the dynamic adaptation of the organism to its environment. Some genes, on this view, do not operate in a static, once and for all fashion. He suggests as an example the functioning of the pituitary–adrenal axis 'not just as the result of past building, but also of present regulating activity of the genes'. He concludes, 'Thus the distinction between hereditary structure determined at conception ... and function as the subsequent response to the environment disappears, and with it, perhaps, the basis for partitioning observed variance into components due to heredity and due to environment.'

It would not be appropriate to pursue this theme here, but its relevance to the future of twin studies is obvious; it is mentioned mainly in order to emphasize that the current resurgence of interest in twin studies is merely a small part of a wider but highly productive approach to the investigation of biological aspects of behaviour. These inquiries are for the most part being undertaken for their intrinsic interest and not, as in the past, out of a polemical preoccupation to deny the influence of social and environmental influences.

They have been made possible by two complementary lines of development; on the one hand psychologists and other behavioural scientists are beginning to refine their terminology by studying specific abilities rather than general ability alone and are also trying to isolate specific environmental variables instead of conceptualizing 'environment' as a broad and somewhat nebulous global construct. At the same time, recent work is characterised by increasingly precise and sophisticated technological advances. Amongst the more important advances relevant to the future of twin studies are more precise methods of diagnosing zygosity, the use of computer-based methods of recording psychophysiological correlates of cognitive processes (e.g. Walter's work, 1969) on the contingent negative variation and Ertl's work (1969) on evoked cortical potential). Furthermore, the rapid development of methods of studying the behaviour and responsiveness of neonates and very young children should make it possible to study newborn twins while they are still relatively innocent of environmental influences – of a social nature at least. It is extraordinary that hardly any studies of newborn twins have been published.

Statistical refinements have also contributed markedly to recent studies in behaviour genetics, and are likely to do so to an increasing extent in the future. Chief among these are multivariate methods of analysis; Cattell's (1965a) Multiple Abstract Variance Analysis (MAVA) is probably the best known but also the method that presents the most formidable data collection difficulties, since information needs to be collected not only on twins but also on parents, siblings and many other relatives. Other multivariate methods involving twins only are described by Bock and Vandenberg in a collection of papers on behaviour genetics edited by Vandenberg (1968a). These methods are mathematically complex, but computer routines for their use on twin data are becoming more widely available. Preliminary results of multivariate analysis of twin differences on the Differential Aptitude Tests have been reported by Bock and Vandenberg (1968).

There is also considerably more scope for the study of separated twins; the total number of separated twins reported in the world literature is not much more than 100. The number of twins born in Britain each year is just under 10,000 pairs. If only 1 per cent of these were separated each year, 100 pairs would be available for study, of whom about one third would be likely to be identical. In a city as large as London, it should not be impossible to trace a reasonable number of twin babies separated at birth or soon after. Ideally, a search for such twins should be made through inspection of records, since it is now obvious that biased samples result from appeals on television. Perhaps such studies are more likely to be made on the continent of Europe where all changes of address have to be officially notified.

But advances in twin studies will by no means be confined to methodological and technological developments alone. More attention is likely to be given to intensive studies of small numbers of twins; in particular more co-twin control studies will probably be reported in the next decade. It is surprising that so little use has been made of the co-twin control method; even Luria and Yudovitch's (1959) well-known study, although well documented, confounded the effects of separation with those of training, while the older studies, such as those of Gesell and Thompson (1929) left much to be desired by comparing the effects of training a skill in one twin with deprivation of training in the other. This design is unsatisfactory, for reasons discussed earlier (see p. 72).

The co-twin method seems to lend itself rather better to a design where two different forms of teaching are compared. A study of this kind has been reported by Naeslund (1956, cited by Vandenberg, 1966). The same method could be extended to attempts to improve specific cognitive skills. This paradigm seems of particular relevance at a time when strenuous attempts are being made to evaluate the effects of pre-school intervention programmes for disadvantaged children. It would not be easy to make the relevant comparisons when one twin was enrolled in a head start programme and the other was simply left at home, since several studies have reported a 'vertical diffusion' effect in which beneficial effects of an enrichment programme extend to other members of the family, and even to other homes in the neighbourhood ('horizontal diffusion', Miller, 1970). However, it may be desirable to compare two different compensatory education methods – for example, one involving a general enrichment programme with the emphasis primarily on activity methods, play and exploration, and the other concentrating perhaps on teaching specific language skills, along the lines advocated by Bereiter and Engelmann (1966). Such studies would inevitably be restricted by a shortage of twins in the community, but an incidence of one in eighty births should not present insuperable obstacles in a large conurbation if appropriate search methods are used. For example, Dencker and Lofving (1958) compared thirty-five twins who had suffered serious head injury with their uninjured co-twins – a less contaminated technique than that used by those who have studied twins discordant for schizophrenia, since in the latter situation both twins have lived in the same environment which may have contributed to the psychosis.

Future twin research is likely to be more concerned with comparisons of learning ability on new tasks or with the differential response to structured teaching situations than with the administration of what are essentially static tests of ability; for example, we might try to compare the response of identical twins to two different methods of accelerating Piagetian concepts of conservation. Different types of instruction might be used for each twin, one stressing comprehension and one merely providing more examples. Here again, results would not be conclusive, mainly because only small samples would be used, but co-twin control experiments might complement more traditional designs with larger numbers. However, it would be necessary to ensure that the twins were really matched on initial levels of ability on the task to be taught.

There is also considerable promise in the use of operant conditioning and behaviour modification techniques with identical twins. These methods already allow the psychologist to use the individual as his own control, rather than constructing 'control groups' of dubious validity (Mittler, 1970b). The child's behaviour is first carefully recorded in order to establish a reliable baseline, after which systematic reinforcement schedules are introduced in order to increase the frequency of the desired behaviour. These methods are now being applied with increasing success in the field of special education (e.g. Bandura, 1969; Bijou and Baer, 1967), but their use within the context of the co-twin control method would be of great interest. For example, it would be instructive to examine intra-pair differences in response to different types and schedules of reinforcement. In general co-twin studies could be productively employed within the wider framework of human behaviour genetics in an effort to elucidate the complex relationship between specific behavioural traits and single or multiple gene effects. This, after all, is one of the major preoccupations of psycho-genetics.

Still at the level of the twin 'couple', we need more information on the twin 'situation'. Despite the many volumes which have been written about twins, we know remarkably little about the psychology of the twin as an individual, or as a member of a pair. A number of useful accounts are available, particularly that of Zazzo (1960); he interviewed a large number of adolescent and adult twin pairs in order to discover something of their reactions to each other, and what it felt like to be a twin. Although a great deal of useful information was collected, we have not so far learned to integrate this kind of material with the construction of the classical type of twin study. There are, for example, many anecdotal accounts of identical twins deliberately seeking different interests and later different occupations in order to escape from the constraints of the twin situation. Similarly, dominance patterns have been described by a number of writers: von Bracken (1939) spoke of one twin tending to act as spokesman to the outside world, while others refer to the secret language and fantasy life of twin pairs during childhood and even extending into adulthood. We also know very little about the way in which parents treat their twins, the extent to which they perceive differences between pairs, or even the extent to which they might be driven to create or exaggerate differences. The only relevant study here is that of Scarr (1968) who showed that it was genetic relatedness rather than perceived similarities that determined similarity of parental treatment (p. 52). More information on the individuality and mutual relationship of the twin pair might well lead to a modification of design in twin studies of the future.

Conclusions

Attempts to identify and study at least some of the determinants of human development and behaviour obviously provide a meeting point for many disciplines – psychology, biology, genetics, education and social studies, to name just a few. None of these disciplines can afford to ignore the rest, and it is only through real collaboration between them that advances can be made. Psychologists certainly cannot expect to tackle these problems on their own, or with the use of exclusively psychological techniques. Indeed, the need for inter-disciplinary research is one of the strongest lessons which has been learned from twin studies.

It is also clear that human behaviour cannot be explained by reference to genetic or environmental factors alone; even in those rare instances where specific genetic mechanisms seem to be involved, as in mongolism or phenylketonuria, genetic disposition towards a given pathology or behaviour can only be expressed in an appropriate environment, whether pre- or post-natal. Although few would now do otherwise than consider these questions in terms of an interaction between genetic and environmental factors, and although we have made a great deal of progress in identifying some of the components involved, we understand very little about the nature or quality of the interactions between them. Up till now, twin studies have tended to emphasize genetic variables in development, mainly because the classical twin studies employing correlational techniques have lent themselves naturally to providing this kind of interpretation. Emphasis on biological variables, although justified by the evidence, should not be regarded as discounting the importance of environment. It is rare to encounter studies in which more than 50 to 60 per cent of the variance is attributable to heredity, but biologically oriented psychologists are usually content to leave it at that, and rarely pursue their investigations to the point where they try to study the precise nature of the environmental contribution, far less the interaction between genetic and environmental factors.

This book has tried to relate twin studies to the broader background of advances in psychology and the developmental sciences, and to indicate some of the reasons why we are likely to see an increasing use of twin studies in the future. These should no longer be seen as the by-product of a fruitless controversy belonging to a previous era, but as contributing an important and unique form of evidence towards the solution of fundamental problems concerning the determinants of growth and development. Only now are we beginning to ask the right questions and to refine our methods of answering them.

Appendix A

Determination of zygosity

Accurate determination of zygosity is an essential procedure in a twin study, but it is generally agreed that complete certainty cannot be achieved. The best that can be attained with careful methods of investigation is about 95 per cent accuracy. Accurate diagnosis is a highly technical and complex process, unfortunately beyond the reach of most psychological investigators, unless they are working in a specialized team with excellent resources.

The main criteria used for discriminating MZ from DZ twins are:

1. Similarity index.
2. Examination of birth membranes.
3. Blood grouping.
4. Palm and finger print analysis (dermatoglyphics).

Similarity index

Some of the earlier twin studies were criticized for using subjective methods of diagnosis, and for designating twins as MZ merely on the basis of identical or strongly similar physical features. The development of dermatoglyphic and serological techniques led to a concentration on these methods, but it has now been shown that impressionistic methods correlate highly with more objective measures. For example, studies in Sweden and the USA indicate that 'diagnosis by questionnaire' could distinguish adult MZ from DZ by the question 'when you were growing up, were you alike as two peas, or was there only a family likeness?'

Where both members of a twin pair had answered this question consistently, over 95 per cent were correctly identified on the evidence of blood and serum grouping (Cederlöf *et al.*, 1961; World Health Organization, 1966).

The main criteria contributing to a similarity index are as follows:

1. Iris pigmentation and pattern.
2. Hair colour, texture and form.
3. Ear size and form.
4. Teeth texture and appearance.
5. Skin texture and colour.
6. General facial similarity.
7. Hand shape.

Examination of birth membranes

Although there is a widespread assumption in both lay and non-specialist medical circles that a single after-birth (placenta) indicated the presence of an MZ pair, it is now clearly established that this is not the case. A distinction has to be made between the placenta (which is all that is visible macroscopically), the chorion (outer bag within the placenta) and the amnion (inner sac). Superficial examination of the placenta is a most unreliable criterion of zygosity, which cannot be determined without more careful examination of the internal membranes, i.e. the chorion and the amnion. It is highly unlikely that placentae would be carefully examined in this way unless there was a special reason to do so – e.g. a research project on twins in the hospital, necessitating accurate zygosity determination. If this were the case, it is likely that blood grouping of cord blood would also be undertaken. For this reason, no reliance can be placed on the statements made by mothers when asked whether there was one placenta or two, since, even if they could recall this detail themselves, statements made by a doctor or midwife about zygosity cannot be accepted as accurate without full examination of the birth membranes.

This fact has been appreciated for many years, but it was

usually assumed that the presence of a single chorion indicated monozygosity. This is now disputed, although thirty years ago Newman, Freeman and Holzinger (1937) drew attention to the possibility of fused dichorial cases being regarded as monochorionic. They also cite German studies of children who were undoubtedly dichorial at birth, but who showed evidence of being MZ in every other characteristic. Gedda (1961), a world authority on the embryology of twinning, reports studies of his own and those of other investigators, which also indicate that DZ twins can be monochorionic. Perhaps the most celebrated instance of dichorial MZ twins were the daughters of the Dutch geneticist and geminologist Waardenburg; their photographs are reproduced in Gedda (1961), together with other instances of monochorionic DZ and dichorionic MZ pairs.

The nature of the foetal membrane is, according to medical opinion, a function of the time interval between fertilization and the splitting of the zygote in MZ twins, and a function of the distance between the two zygotes in the case of DZs. When the original egg divides almost immediately after fertilization, the two halves pull apart and become implanted in different sites of the uterus. Each embryo is then likely to develop separately from the other, and has its own placenta, chorion and amnion. Scheinfeld (1968) cites evidence that up to 30 per cent of identicals develop in this way. In the majority of identicals, however, the egg divides after it has begun to develop, and the two parts, although separate, stay close enough together to grow within the same chorion attached to the same placenta.

These considerations are important not only from the point of view of accurate zygosity determination, but also in relation to the whole intra-uterine developmental process.

Blood grouping

Detailed comparison of blood groups is now considered an important and highly reliable method of zygosity determination, though there are difficulties involved in taking blood samples from young children. Full blood group analysis and grouping requires a specialized laboratory to isolate the large number of substances that need to be compared; apart from the ABO groups and the rhesus factor, which can easily be examined by any hospital pathology laboratory, accurate zygosity determination involves a much more detailed study of the 'M' and 'N' substances, and about twenty-six additional substances such as 'S', 'P', 'Kell', 'Duffy', 'Lewis'.

Palm and finger print analysis

Dermatoglyphic analysis is widely used in zygosity determination, and, together with blood analysis, constitutes the most reliable method. When both methods are used, the probability of an incorrect diagnosis is very small.

There is conclusive evidence that finger and palm prints are not only genetically determined, but laid down at a very early stage of foetal development, and not thereafter subject to changes of an environmental nature. The extensive studies of Dr Sarah Holt of the Galton Laboratory, University of London, have shown how closely the observed MZ and DZ intraclass correlations fit the theoretical expecta-

Table 30

Theoretical and Observed Correlations for Total Finger Ridge Count

	Theoretical	*Holt*	*Huntley*
MZ twins	1·00	0·95	0·96
DZ twins	0·50	0·49	0·49
Sib–sib	0·50	0·50	0·51
Parent–child	0·50	0·48	0·43
Midparent–child	0·71	0·66	0·62
Husband–wife	0·00	0·05	0·01

Sources: Holt (1961); Huntley (1966)

tions for a characteristic determined by polygenic inheritance alone (Holt, 1961). They have the additional advantage of not being subject to assortative mating.

Table 30 shows the theoretical correlations which would be predicted from such a polygenic model, and compares the actual correlations obtained by Holt (1961) and also by Huntley (1966) in a study of 320 twins and their parents and siblings.

Appendix B

Heritability estimates

Various attempts have been made to quantify the extent to which a characteristic is genetic in origin or, more precisely, what proportion of the variation between individuals can be ascribed to genetic factors. Heritability ratios or indices vary widely in aim and outcome, and have all been regarded with suspicion by behaviour geneticists and environmentalists alike, though for different reasons. The latter object to any quantitative ratio as such, while the former are divided about the assumptions underlying a particular formula. Before reviewing some of the main indices that have been proposed, it may be reassuring to point out that several recent studies have shown substantial agreement between heritability estimates when a series of tests are placed in rank order, even though absolute values of the various indices might differ considerably. In an analysis of data from the Illinois Test of Psycholinguistic Abilities, for example, it was shown that four different indices produced virtually identical results when the nine sub-tests were placed in rank order (Mittler, 1969b).

Heritability indices – usually collectively known as h^2 – represent attempts to partition the variance into its genetic and environmental components; they are usually based on the comparison of intraclass correlations between identical and fraternal pairs.

The intraclass correlation coefficient r_i is derived by the analysis of variance method described by Fuller and Thompson (1960). The formula is

$$r_i = \frac{\Sigma (x_i - a)(y_i - a)}{ns^2} = \frac{\Sigma x_i y_i - na^2}{ns^2},$$

where $x_i y_i$ is the measurement on the ith pair of twins,

$\quad n$ is the number of pairs

$\quad s^2$ is the variance of total sample about a

$\quad a$ is the mean of all measurements.

This correlation is interpreted as 'the total variance minus proportion of the total variance which arises from the fact that twin pairs differ from each other' (p. 113). The intraclass correlation is calculated by analysis of variance, and therefore yields an F-ratio which needs to be significant if the correlation is to be interpreted meaningfully.

Heritability has been defined in the narrow sense by Falconer (1960) as 'the ratio of additive genetic variance to phenotypic variance', and refers to the population as a whole. The total phenotypic variance can be regarded as the sum total of variance due to genetic and to environmental factors. It can be partitioned into variance *within* and variance *between* pairs of twins.

One of the earliest and most widely used ratios was Holzinger's H. He proposed two alternative formulae, one based on within-pair variances only, and the other on the intraclass correlation:

$$H = \frac{\text{var}_{DZ} - \text{var}_{MZ}}{\text{var}_{DZ}},$$

$$H = \frac{r_{MZ} - r_{DZ}}{1 - r_{DZ}}.$$

The second formula has been widely used, but has been criticized on several grounds, mainly because it is limited to a comparison of within-pair variances, and takes no account of between-pair variances. More precisely, it subtracts the non-genetic component, estimated from the MZ within-pair variance, from the within-pair DZ variance, and thus gives an estimate of the proportion of the total DZ variance which is due to genetic differences between twins. As Huntley points out,

this is not the same as estimating the heritability of a characteristic in the general population, because the genetic variance within pairs of DZ twins is only half that between unrelated people, while the environmental variance within pairs may be less, or the same, or even more than that between unrelated people (Huntley, 1969, personal communication).

More recent heritability indices, such as that by Falconer (1960), aim to estimate the extent to which a characteristic is genetically determined in the general population. Falconer's argument is described by Huntley (1966) thus:

For MZ twins all the additive genetic variance will be between-pairs because there are no unshared genes to cause differences within-pairs. . . . Differences within the pairs will be environmental differences. But if these environmental differences within pairs are less than the total environmental variance in the population, there will be a portion of this total variance which is common to members of the twin pairs and is an additional cause of similarity between them.

MZ and DZ twins, by virtue of being two children of the same age growing up in the same family at the same time, may be assumed in general to be subject to much the same degree of environmental differences and similarities. Hence, in partitioning the variance for DZ twins, the within-pair environmental variance component and the between-pair common environmental variance component will be the same as for MZ twins. However, DZ twins are on average genetically only half alike, so half the additive genetic variance will be within-pairs, and half between-pairs. . . . The differences between the between-pair components for MZ and DZ twins, which is the same as the difference between the covariances of the two kinds of twins, will be equal to half the genetic variance in the population . . . (p. 237–8).

Table 31, adapted from Falconer (1960), summarizes the above argument and shows how the components of the variance between and within pairs of twins may be partitioned.

Table 31

Partitioning of Components of Variance between and within Pairs of Twins

	Between pairs	*Within pairs*
MZ twins	$V_g + V_{ec}$	V_{ew}
DZ twins	$\frac{1}{2}V_g + V_{ec}$	$\frac{1}{2}V_g + V_{ew}$
Difference	$\frac{1}{2}V_g$	$\frac{1}{2}V_g$

where V_g = additive genetic variance.

V_{ec} = variance between pairs due to common environment between pairs.

V_{ew} = variance due to environmental differences between pairs.

Source: Falconer (1960)

The derivation of a heritability formula follows from this argument. Since the difference between r_{MZ} and r_{DZ} constitutes half the genetic variance, the total genetic variance is given by the formula

$$h^2 = 2(r_{MZ} - r_{DZ}).$$

Three other formulae have also been proposed recently by Jensen (1967), Nichols (1965) and Vandenberg (1965). Jensen's formula is virtually identical to Falconer's, but is notable for the addition of some important refinements such as an estimate of the proportion of the total variance due to systematic (between families) environmental differences (E^2), and also due to unsystematic (within families) environmental variance (e^2). His h^2 formula is essentially

$$h^2 = \frac{r_{MZ} - r_{DZ}}{1 - r_{sg}},$$

where r_{sg} = the genetic correlation between siblings. Since r_{sg} is normally 0·50, the formula becomes identical to Falconer's

$$h^2 = \frac{r_{MZ} - r_{DZ}}{0 \cdot 50}.$$

Nichols (1965) has proposed a formula for the heritability ratio (HR) as follows:

$$HR = \frac{2(r_{MZ} - r_{DZ})}{r_{MZ}}.$$

Finally, Vandenberg (1965) recommends the use of the F-ratio to evaluate the statistical significance of the ratio between the fraternal and identical within-pair variance

$$F = \frac{v_{DZ}}{v_{MZ}},$$

and demonstrates that F and H as calculated by Holzinger's original formula are related in the following way:

$$F = \frac{1}{1 - H}.$$

Vandenberg (1966) points out that these conversion formulae are useful in comparing results obtained from studies using different methods. Unfortunately, different methods yield different absolute heritability values, as the following table, adapted from Jensen (1967), indicates.

Table 32

Comparison of Holzinger's H, Nichols's HR and Jensen's h^2 for different values of r

r_{MZ}	r_{DZ}	H	HR	h^2
1·00	0·50	1·00	1·00	1·00
0·40	0·20	0·25	1·00	0·40
0·90	0·80	0·50	0·22	0·20
1·00	0·99	1·00	0·02	0·02

Source: Jensen (1967)

Jensen's calculations reproduced in the above table indicate that H, HR and h^2 are not monotonic functions of one another. Nevertheless, as already pointed out, the various ratios often produce very similar results when a set of tests is placed in rank order of h^2.

References

AMBROSE, A. (1961), 'The development of the smiling response in early infancy', in B. M. Foss (ed.), *Determinants of Infant Behaviour*, Tavistock.

BANDURA, A. (1969), *Principles of Behavior Modification*, Holt, Rinehart & Winston.

BAYLEY, N. (1954), 'Some increasing parent–child similarities during the growth of children', *J. educ. Psychol.*, vol. 45, pp. 1–21.

BAYLEY, N. (1956), 'Individual patterns of development', *Child Devel.*, vol. 27, pp. 45–74.

BENE, E. (1965), 'On the genesis of male homosexuality', *Brit. J. Psychiat.*, vol. 111, pp. 803–13.

BEREITER, C., and ENGELMANN, S. (1966). *Teaching Disadvantaged Children in the Pre-School*, Prentice-Hall.

BERG, J. M. (1965), 'Aetiological aspects of mental subnormality: pathological factors,' in A. and A.D.B. Clarke (eds.), *Mental Deficiency: The Changing Outlook*, 2nd edn, Methuen.

BERG, J. M., and KIRMAN, B. (1960), 'The mentally defective twin', *Brit. med. J.*, vol. 1, pp. 1190–92.

BERNSTEIN, B. (1965),'A socio-linguistic approach to learning', in J. Gould (ed.), *Penguin Survey of Social Sciences*, Penguin Books.

BIJOU, S. W., and BAER, D. M. (1967), 'Operant methods in child behavior and development', in S. W. Bijou and D. M. Baer (eds.), *Child Development: Readings in Experimental Analysis*, Appleton-Century-Crofts.

BIRCH, H. G., and TIZARD, J. (1967), 'The dietary treatment of phenylketonuria: not proven?', *Devel. Med. child Neurol.* vol. 9, pp. 9–12.

BLAU, A., WELKOWITZ, J., and COHEN, J. (1964), 'Maternal attitude to pregnancy instrument', *Arch. gen. Psychiat.*, vol. 10, pp. 324–31.

BLEULER, M. (1968), 'A twenty-three year longitudinal study of 208 schizophrenics and impressions in regard to the nature of schizophrenia', *J. psychiat, Res.*, vol. 6, pp. 3–24.

BLEWETT, D. B. (1954), 'An experimental study of the inheritance of intelligence', *J. ment. Sci.*, vol. 100, pp. 922–33.

BLOCK, J. B. (1968), 'Hereditary components in the performance of twins on the WAIS', in S. G. Vandenberg (ed.), *Progress in Human Behavior Genetics*, Johns Hopkins Press.

BOCK, D. B. and VANDENBERG, S. G. (1968), 'Components of heritable variation in mental test scores', in S. G. Vandenberg (ed.), *Progress in Human Behavior Genetics*, Johns Hopkins Press.

BÖÖK, J. A. (1953), 'Oligophrenia', in A. Sorsby (ed.), *Clinical Genetics*, Butterworth.

BOWLBY, J. (1957), 'An ethological approach to research in child development,' *Brit. J. med. Psychol.*, vol. 30, pp. 230–40.

BRACKEN, H. von (1939), 'Untersuchungen an Zwillingen über die Entwicklung der Selbständigkeit im Kindesalter', *Arch. ges. Psychol.*, vol. 105, pp. 217–42.

BRACONI, Z. (1961), 'Le psiconeurosi e le psicosi nei gemelli', *Acta genet. Med.*, vol. 10, pp. 100–36.

BRANDON, W. M. G., KIRMAN, B. H., and WILLIAMS, C. E. (1959), 'Microcephaly in one of monozygotic twins', *Arch. dis. Child.*, vol. 34, pp. 56–9.

BRODY, D. (1937), 'Twin resemblances in mechanical ability, with reference to the effects of practice on performance', *Child Devel.*, vol. 8, pp. 207–16.

BROWN, A. M., STAFFORD, R. E., and VANDENBERG, S. G. (1967), 'Twins: behavioral differences', *Child Devel.*, vol. 38, pp. 1055–64.

BRUUN, K. T., MARKANEN, T., and PARTANEN, J. (1966), *Inheritance of Drinking Behaviour: A Study of Adult Twins*, Finnish Foundation for Alcohol Research.

BURLINGHAM, D. (1952), *Twins: A Study of Three Pairs of Identical Twins*, Imago.

BURT, C. (1966), 'The genetic determination of differences in intelligence: a study of monozygotic twins reared together and apart', *Brit. J. Psychol.*, vol. 57, pp. 137–53.

CANTER, S. (1969), 'Personality traits in twins', unpublished paper delivered to annual conference of the British Psychological Society.

CARR-SAUNDERS, A. M., and JONES, D. (1937), *A Survey of the Social Structure of England and Wales*, Clarendon Press.

CARTER, C. O. (1966), 'Differential fertility by intelligence', in J. E. Meade and A. S. Parkes (eds.), *Genetic and Environmental Factors in Human Ability*, Oliver & Boyd.

CARTER, H. D. (1933), 'Twin similarities in personality traits', *J. genet. Psychol.*, vol. 43, pp. 312–21.

CATTELL, R. B. (1965a), 'Methodological and conceptual advances in evaluating hereditary and environmental influences and their interaction', in S. G. Vandenberg (ed.), *Methods and Goals in Human Behavior Genetics*, Academic Press.

174 References

CATTELL, R. B. (1965b), *The Scientific Study of Personality*, Penguin Books.

CEDERLÖF, R., FRIEBERG, L., JONSON, E., and KAIJ, L. (1961), 'Studies on similarity diagnosis in twins, with the aid of mailed questionnaires', *Acta genet.*, vol. 11, pp. 338–62.

CLARIDGE, G., *Psychophysiological and Psychological Factors in Twins*, in press.

CLARKE, L. G., and HARDING, F. A. (1969), 'Comparisons of mono and dizygotic twins with respect to some features of the electroencephalogram', *Proc. electrophysiol. technol. Assoc.*, vol. 16, pp. 94–101.

CORNEY, G., and AHERNE, W. (1965), 'The placental transfusion syndrome in twins', *Arch. dis. Child.*, vol. 40, pp. 264–70.

DARLINGTON, C. D. (1954), 'Heredity and environment', *Caryologia*, vol. 190, pp. 370–81.

DARLINGTON, C. D. (1963), 'Psychology, genetics and the process of history', *Brit. J. Psychol.*, vol. 54, pp. 292–9.

DAVIS, D. R. (1966), *An Introduction to Psychopathology*, 2nd edn, Oxford University Press.

DAVIS, E. A. (1937), 'The development of linguistic skill in twins, singletons and sibs, and only children from five to ten', *Univ. Minnesota Inst. Child Welf.*, monogr. 14.

DAY, E. (1932), 'The development of language in twins: a comparison of twins and single children', *Child Devel.*, vol. 3, pp. 179–99.

DAY, E. (1932), 'The development of twins: their resemblances and differences', *Child Devel.*, vol. 3, pp. 298–316.

DENCKER, S. J., and LOFVING, B. (1958), 'A psychometric study of identical twins discordant for head injury', *Acta psychol. neurol. Scand.*, vol. 33, supp. 122.

DENNIS, W. (1941), 'Infant development under restricted practice and minimum social stimulation', *Genet. psychol. Monogrs.*, vol. 23, pp. 142–91.

DOLL, E. A. (1953), *The Measurement of Social Competence*, Education Testing Bureau.

DOUGLAS, J. W. B. (1964), *The Home and the School*, MacGibbon & Kee.

DOUGLAS, J. W. B. (1968), *All Our Future*, Peter Davies.

DRILLIEN, C. M. (1964), *The Growth and Development of Prematurely Born Children*, Livingstone.

DUNN, P. (1965), 'Some perinatal observations on twins', *Devel. Med. child Neurol.*, vol. 7, pp. 121–34.

DUSTMAN, R. E., and BECK, E. C. (1965), 'The visually evoked potential in twins', *EEG Clin. Neurophysiol.*, vol. 19, pp. 570–75.

ERLENMEYER-KIMLING, L., and JARVIK, L. F. (1963), 'Genetics and intelligence', *Science*, vol. 142, pp. 1477–9.

ERTL, J. (1969), 'Evoked potentials, neural efficiency and IQ', in L. D. Proctor (ed.), *Biocybernetics of the Central Nervous System*, Atlantic-Little, Brown.

ESSEN-MOLLER, E. (1941), 'Psychiatrische Untersuchungen in einer Serie von Zwillingen', *Acta psychiat.*, supp. 23.

EYSENCK, H. J. (1956), 'The inheritance of intraversion–extraversion', *Acta Psychol.*, vol. 12, pp. 95–110.

EYSENCK, H. J. (1964), *Crime and Personality*, Routledge & Kegan Paul.

EYSENCK, H. J. (1967a), *The Biological Basis of Personality*, Charles C. Thomas.

EYSENCK, H. J. (1967b), 'Intelligence assessment : a theoretical and experimental approach', *Brit. J. educ. Psychol.*, vol. 37, pp. 81–98.

EYSENCK, H. J., and PRELL, D. B. (1951), 'The inheritance of neuroticism', *J. ment. Sci.*, vol. 97, pp. 447–65.

FALCONER, D. S. (1960), *Introduction to Quantitative Genetics*, Oliver & Boyd.

FISCHER, M., HARVARD, B., and HAUGE, M. (1969), 'A Danish twin study of schizophrenia', *Brit. J. Psychiat.*, vol. 115, pp. 981–90.

FLAVELL, J. (1963), *The Developmental Psychology of Jean Piaget*, Van Nostrand.

FOX, H., GIFFORD, S., VALENSTEIN, A. F., and MURAWSKI, B. J. (1965), 'Psychophysiology of male monozygotic twins', *Arch. gen. Psychiat.*, vol. 12, pp. 490–500.

FOX, H., GIFFORD, S., VALENSTEIN, A. F., and MURAWSKI, B. J. (1970), 'Psychophysiological correlation of seventeen ketosteroids and seventeen hydroxycosteroids in twenty-one pairs of monozygotic twins', *J. psychosomatic Res.*, vol. 14, pp. 71–9.

FRASER, E. D. (1959), *Home Environment and the School*, University of London Press.

FREEDMAN, D. G. (1965), 'An ethological approach to the genetical study of human behavior', in S. G. Vandenberg (ed.), *Methods and Goals in Human Behavior Genetics*, Academic Press.

FROSTIG, M., LEFEVER, D. W. and WHITTLESEY, J. R. B. (1964), *Marianne Frostig Developmental Test of Visual Perception*, Consulting Psychologists Press.

FULLER, L. J., and THOMPSON, W. R. (1960), *Behavior Genetics*, Wiley.

GALTON, F. (1875), 'The history of twins as a criterion of the relative powers of nature and nurture', *Fraser's Magazine*, vol. 12, pp. 566–76.

GALTON, F. (1883), *Inquiries into Human Faculty and Its Development*, Macmillan.

GARN, S. M. (1966), 'The evolutionary and genetic control of variability in man', *Annals N.Y. Acad. Sci.*, vol. 134, pp. 602–15.

GEDDA, L. (1961), *Twins in History and in Science*, Charles C. Thomas.

GESELL, A. L., and THOMPSON, H. (1929), 'Learning and growth in identical infant twins', *Genet. psychol. Monogrs.*, vol. 6, pp. 5–120.

GESELL, A. L., and THOMPSON, H. (1941), 'Twins T and C from infancy to adolescence: a biogenetic study of individual differences by the method of co-twin control', *Genet. psychol. Monogrs.*, vol. 24.

GOLDBERG, E. M., and MORRISON, S. L. (1963), 'Schizophrenia and social class', *Brit. J. Psychiat.*, vol. 109, pp. 785–802.

GOLDBERG, E. M. (1968), 'The families of schizophrenic patients', in H. Freeman and J. Farndale (eds.), *New Aspects of the Mental Health Services*, Pergamon.

GOTTESMAN, I. I. (1963), 'Genetic aspects of intelligent behavior', in N. R. Ellis (ed.), *Handbook of Mental Deficiency*, McGraw-Hill.

GOTTESMAN, I. I. (1965), 'Personality and natural selection', in S. G. Vandenberg (ed.), *Methods and Goals in Human Behavior*, Academic Press.

GOTTESMAN, I. I. (1966), 'Genetic variance in an adaptive personality trait', *J. child Psychol. and Psychiat.*, vol. 7, pp. 199–208.

GOTTESMAN, I. I., and SHIELDS, J. (1966), 'Schizophrenia in twins: sixteen years consecutive admissions to a psychiatric clinic', *Brit. J. Psychiat.*, vol. 112, pp. 809–18.

GOUGH, H. G. (1965), 'The adjective check list as a personality research technique', *Psychol. reports*, vol. 6, pp. 107–22.

GRIFFITHS, D. R. (1970), 'Assessment of personality', in P. Mittler (ed.), *Psychological Assessment of Mental and Physical Handicaps*, Methuen.

HALSEY, A. H. (1959), 'Class differences in intelligence', *Brit. J. stat. Psychol.*, vol. 12, pp. 1–4

HARLOW, H. (1963), 'The maternal–affectional system', in B. M. Foss (ed.), *Determinants of Infant Behaviour*, vol. 2, Tavistock.

HARVALD, B., and HAUGE, M. (1965), 'Hereditary factors elucidated by twin studies', in J. V. Neel, M. W. Shaw and W. J. Schull (eds.), *Genetics and the Epidemiology of Chronic Diseases*, US Department of Health, Education & Welfare.

HEBB, D. O. (1949), *The Organization of Behavior*, Wiley.

HESTON, L. L. (1966), 'Psychiatric disorders in foster-home reared children of schizophrenic mothers', *Brit. J. Psychiat.*, vol. 112, pp. 819–25.

HESTON, L. L., and DENNY, D. (1968), 'Interactions between early life experience and biological factors in schizophrenia', *J. psychiat. Res.*, vol. 6, pp. 363–76.

HESTON, L. L., and SHIELDS, J. (1968), 'Homosexuality in twins', *Arch. genet. Psychiat.*, vol. 18, pp. 149–60.

HILGARD, J. R. (1933), 'The effect of early and delayed practice on memory and motor performance studied by the method of co-twin control', *Genet. psychol. Monogrs.*, no. 14, pp. 493–567.

HINDEN, E. (1956), 'Idiocy in one of monozygotic twins', *Brit. med. J.*, vol. 1, p. 333.

HIRSCH, K. de, JANSKY, J. J., and LANGFORD, W. S. (1964), 'The oral language and performance of premature children and controls', *J. sp. hear. Disorders*, vol. 29, pp. 60–69.

HOLT, S. B. (1961), 'Inheritance of dermal ridge patterns', in L. S. Penrose (ed.), *Recent Advances in Human Genetics*, Churchill.

HUME, W. I. (1969), 'Psychological and perceptual indices of responsiveness in twins', unpublished paper presented to annual conference of British Psychological Society.

HUNTLEY, R. M. C. (1966), 'A study of 320 twin pairs and their families showing resemblances in respect of a number of physical and psychological measurements', University of London, unpublished Ph.D. thesis.

HURST, L. A. (1965), 'Genetic factors', in B. Wolman (ed.), *Handbook of Clinical Psychology*, McGraw-Hill.

HUSÉN, T. (1953), *Twillingstudier*, Almqvist & Wiksell.

HUSÉN, T. (1959), *Psychological Twin Research*, Almqvist & Wiksell.

HUSÉN, T. (1961), 'Abilities of twins', *Acta Psychol.*, vol. 19, pp. 1–2.

HUSÉN, T. (1963), 'Intra-pair similarities in the school achievements of twins', *Scand. J. Psychol.*, vol. 4, pp. 108–14.

IHDA, S. (1961), 'A study of neurosis by twin method', *Psychiat. Neurol. Jap.*, vol. 63, pp. 861–92.

INGRAM, T. T. S. (1965), 'Specific retardation of speech development', *Speech Path. and Speech Therapy*, vol. 8, pp. 1–12.

INOUYE, E. (1961), 'Similarity and dissimilarity of schizophrenia in twins', *Proc. 3rd World Cong. Psychiat*, University of Toronto Press and McGill Press.

INOUYE, E. (1965), 'Similar and dissimilar manifestations of obsessive–compulsive neurosis in monozygotic twins', *Amer. J. Psychiat.*, vol. 121, pp. 1171–5.

JARVIK, L. F., KALLMAN, F. J., and KLABER, M. M. (1957), 'Changing intellectual functions in senescent twins', *Acta. genet. et Statist. med.*, vol. 7, pp. 421–30.

JENSEN, A. R. (1967), 'Estimation of the limits of heritability of traits by comparison of monozygotic and dizygotic twins', *Proc. Nat. Acad. Sci.*, vol. 58, pp. 149–56.

JENSEN, A. R. (1969), 'How much can we boost IQ and scholastic achievement?', *Harvard educ. Rev.*, vol. 39, pp. 1–123.

JINKS, J. L., and FULKER, D. W. (1970), 'A comparison of biometrical, genetical, MAVA and the classical approaches to the analysis of human behavior', *Psychol. Bull.*, vol. 73, pp. 311–49.

JOST, H., and SONTAG, L. (1944), 'The genetic factor in autonomic nervous system function', *Psychosomatic Med.*, vol. 6, pp. 308–10.

JUEL-NIELSEN, N., and HARVALD, B. (1958), 'The EEG in uniovular twins brought up apart', *Acta genet.*, vol. 8, pp. 57–64.

KAGAN, J., and MOSS, H. (1962), *From Birth to Maturity*, Wiley.

KALLMANN, F. J. (1946), 'The genetic theory of schizophrenia: an analysis of 691 schizophrenic twin index families', *Amer. J. Psychiat.*, vol. 103, pp. 309–22.

KALLMANN, F. J. (1952), 'Comparative twin study on the genetic aspects of male homosexuality', *J. nerv. ment. Diseases*, vol. 115, pp. 283–98.

KALLMANN, F. J. (1953), *Heredity in Health and Mental Disorder*, Chapman & Hall.

KALLMANN, F. J., and ROTH, B. (1956), 'Genetic aspects of pre-adolescent schizophrenia', *Amer. J. Psychiat.*, vol. 112, pp. 599–606.

KAPLAN, B. (1954), 'Environmental and human plasticity', *Amer. Anthropol.*, vol. 50, pp. 780–800.

KETY, S., ROSENTHAL, D., WENDER, P., and SCHULSINGER, F. (1968), 'The types and prevalence of mental illness in the biological and adoptive families of adopted schizophrenics', *J. psychiat. Res.*, vol. 6, supp. 1, pp. 345–62.

KIRK, S. A., MCCARTHY, J. J., and KIRK, W. (1968), *The Illinois Test of Psycholinguistic Abilities*, rev. edn, Institute for Research in Exceptional Children.

KOCH, H. L. (1966), *Twins and Twin Relations*, Chicago University Press.

KOHLER, W. (1925), *The Mentality of Apes*, Harcourt, Brace & World.

KOHN, M. L. (1968), 'Social class and schizophrenia', *J. psychiat. Res.*, vol. 6, supp. 1, pp. 155–74.

KRINGLEN, E. (1964), 'Schizophrenia in male monozygotic twins', *Acta Psychiat.*, suppl. 178.

KRYSHOVA, N. A., BELIAEVA, Z. V., DMITRIEVA, A. F., ZHILINSKAIE, M. A., and PERNOV, L. G. (1963), 'Investigation of higher nervous activity and certain vegetative features in twins', *Soviet Psychol. Psychiat.*, vol. 1, pp. 36–41.

LAING, R. D., and ESTERSON, H. (1965), *Sanity, Madness and the Family*, Tavistock.

LANG, R. (1940), 'Studies on the genetic determination of homosexuality', *J. nerv. ment. Diseases*, vol. 92, pp. 55–64.

LAUTERBACH, C. E. (1925), 'Studies in twin resemblance', *Genetics*, vol. 10, pp. 525–68.

LEHTOVAARA, A., SAARINEN, P., and JARVINEN, J. (1965), *Psychological Studies of Twins: 1. GSR Reactions*, Psychological Institute, University of Helsinki.

LENNEBERG, E. H. (1967), *Biological Foundations of Language*, Wiley.

LENNOX, W. G., GIBBS, E. L., and GIBBS, F. A. (1954), 'The inheritance of epilepsy as revealed by the electroencephalogram', *J. Heredity*, vol. 36, pp. 233–43.

LEY, P. (1970), 'Acute psychiatric patients', in P. Mittler (ed.), *The Psychological Assessment of Mental and Physical Handicaps*, Methuen.

LIDZ, T. (1968), 'The family, language and the transmission of schizophrenia', *J. psychiat. Res.*, vol. 6, supp. 1, pp. 175–84.

LIPSITT, L. (1966), 'Learning processes of human newborns', *Merrill-Palmer Q.*, vol. 12, pp. 45–71.

LIPTON, E. L., STEINSCHNEIDER, A., and RICHMOND, J. B. (1966), 'Psychophysiologic disorders in children', in L. W. and M. L. Hoffman (eds.), *Review of Child Development Research*, vol. 2, Russell Sage Foundation.

LURIA, A. R., and YUDOVITCH, F. I. (1959), *Speech and the Development of Mental Processes in the Child* (ed. J. Simon), Staples.

LUXENBURGER, H. (1928), 'Vorläufiger Bericht über psychiatrische Serienuntersuchungen an Zwillingen', *Z. ges. Neurol. Psychiat.*, vol. 116, pp. 297–326.

LUXENBURGER, H. (1942), 'Das zirkulare Irresein', in A. Gutt (ed.), *Handbuch der Erbkrankeiten*, Thieme.

MCCARTHY, D. (1930), 'The language development of the pre-school child', *Univ. Minnesota Inst. Child Welf.*, monogr. 4.

MCCARTHY, J. J., and KIRK, S. A. (1961), *The Illinois Test of Psycholinguistic Abilities*, Institute for Research in Exceptional Children.

MCGRAW, M. (1935), *Growth: A Study of Johnny and Judy*, Appleton-Century-Crofts.

MCLEAN, G. (1964), 'Genetics and behaviour development' in W. L. Hoffman and M. Hoffman (eds.), *Review of Child Development Research*, Russell Sage Foundation.

MCMAHON, B. (1968), 'Gene-environment interaction in human disease', *J. psychiat. Res.*, vol. 6, supp. 1, pp. 393–402.

MCNEMAR, Q. (1933), 'Twin resemblances in motor skills and the effect of practice thereon', *J. genet. Psychol.*, vol. 42, pp. 70–97.

MCSWEENEY, D. A. (1970), 'A report on a pair of monozygotic twins discordant for schizophrenia', *Brit. J. Psychiat.*, vol. 116, pp. 315–22.

MARKS, I. M., CROWE, M., DREWE, E., YOUNG, J., and
DEWHURST, W. G. (1969), 'Obsessive–compulsive neurosis in
identical twins', *Brit. J. Psychiat.*, vol. 115, pp. 991–8.

MEISSNER, M. W. (1965), 'Functional and adaptive aspects of
cellular regulatory mechanisms', *Psychol. Bull.*, vol. 64, pp. 206–17.

MERRIMAN, C. (1924), 'The intellectual resemblance of twins',
Psychol. monogr. 33 (5).

MEYERS, C. E., ORPERT, R. E., ATTWELL, A. A., and
DINGMAN, H. F. (1962), 'Primary mental abilities at mental
age six', *Monogr. Soc. Res. child Devel.*, vol. 27, no. 1,
whole no. 82.

MILLER, J. O. (1970), 'Cultural deprivation and its modification',
in C. Haywood (ed.), *Socio-Cultural Aspects of Mental
Retardation*, Appleton-Century-Crofts.

MIRENVA, A. N. (1935), 'Psychomotor education and the general
development of pre-school children', *Pedagogical Seminary and
J. genet. Psychol.*, vol. 46, pp. 433–54.

MITTLER, P. (1969a), 'Psycholinguistic skills in four-year-old twins
and singletons', Ph.D. thesis, University of London.

MITTLER, P. (1969b), 'Genetic aspects of psycholinguistic abilities',
J. child Psychol. and Psychiat., vol. 10, pp. 165–76.

MITTLER, P. (ed.) (1970a), *The Psychological Assessment of
Mental and Physical Handicaps*, Methuen.

MITTLER, P. (1970b), 'New directions in the study of learning
disorders', in A. D. B. Clarke (ed.), *Learning Processes in the
Mentally Subnormal*, Tavistock.

MITTLER, P. (1970c), 'Biological and social aspects of language
development in twins', *Devel. Med. child Neurol.*, vol. 12,
pp. 741–57.

MITTLER, P., and WARD, J. (1970), 'The use of the Illinois Test of
Psycholinguistic Abilities with English four-year-old children:
a normative and factorial study', *Brit. J. educ. Psychol.*, vol. 40,
pp. 43–53.

NAESLUND, J. (1956), *Metodiken vid den Första Läsundervisningen:
– Oversikt och Experimentella Bidrag*, Svenska Bokförlaget
Norstedts.

NEEL, J. V., and SCHULL, W. J. (1954), *Human Heredity*, Chicago
University Press.

NEILON, P. (1948), 'Shirley's babies after fifteen years: a personality
study', *J. genet. Psychol.*, vol. 73, pp. 175–86.

NEWMAN, H. W. (1923), *The Physiology of Twinning*, University
of Chicago Press.

NEWMAN, H. H., FREEMAN, F. N., and HOLZINGER, K. J.
(1937), *Twins: A Study of Heredity and Environment*, University
of Chicago Press.

NEWSON, J., and NEWSON, E. (1968), *Four Years Old in an
Urban Community*, Allen & Unwin; Penguin Books 1970.

NICHOLS, R. C. (1965), 'The national merit twin study', in S. G. Vandenberg (ed.), *Methods and Goals in Human Behavior Genetics*, Academic Press.

NICHOLS, R. C., and SCHNELL, R. R. (1963), 'Factor scales for the California Personality Inventory', *J. consult. Psychol.*, vol. 27, pp. 228–35.

OSBORNE, R. T., and GREGOR, J. A. (1966), 'The heritability of visualization, perceptual speed and spatial orientation', *Perc. mot. Skills*, vol. 23, pp. 379–90.

OSBORNE, R. T., GREGOR, J. A., and MIELE, F. (1967), 'Heritability of numerical facility', *Perc. mot. Skills*, vol. 24, pp. 659–66.

OSBORNE, R. T., GREGOR, J. A., and MIELE, F. (1968), 'Heritability of factor V: verbal comprehension', *Perc. mot. Skills*, vol. 26, pp. 191–202.

OSGOOD, C. E. (1957), 'A behaviouristic analysis', in C. E. Osgood (ed.), *Contemporary Approaches to Cognition*, Harvard University Press.

PARKER, N. (1966), 'Twin relationships and concordance for neurosis', *Proceedings of the Fourth World Congress of Psychiatry*, Excerpta Medica.

PENROSE, L. S. (1963), *The Biology of Mental Defect*, 3rd edn, Sidgwick & Jackson.

PETRI, E. (1934), 'Untersuchungen zur Erbedingtheit der Menarche', *Z. morph. Anthr.*, vol. 33, pp. 43–8.

PIAGET, J. (1926), *Language and Thought of the Child*, Routledge & Kegan Paul.

PIAGET, J. (1951), *Play, Dreams and Imitation in Childhood*, Heinemann.

PICKFORD, R. W. (1951), *Individual Differences in Colour Vision*, Routledge & Kegan Paul.

PIRE, G. (1966), 'Application des techniques sociométriques à l'étude des jumeaux', *Enfance*, vol. 1, pp. 23–48.

PLOWDEN REPORT (1967), *Children and their Primary Schools*, Central Advisory Council for Education, HMSO.

POLLIN, W., and STABENAU, J. R. (1968), 'Biological, psychological and historical differences in a series of monozygotic twins discordant for schizophrenia', *J. psychiat. Res.*, vol. 6, supp. 1, pp. 317–32.

POLLIN, W., ALLEN, M., HEFFER, A., STABENAU, J., and HRUBEC, Z. (1969), 'Psychopathology in 15,909 pairs of veteran twins: evidence for a genetic factor in their pathogenesis of schizophrenia and its relative absence in psychoneurosis', *Amer. J. Psychiat.*, vol. 126, pp. 597–610.

PRICE, B. (1950), 'Primary biases in twin studies', *Amer. J. hum. Genet.*, vol. 2, pp. 293–352.

PRINGLE, M. K., BUTLER, N., and DAVIE, R. (1966), *Eleven Thousand Seven-Year-Olds*, Longmans.

RECORD, R. G., McKEOWN, T., and EDWARDS, J. H. (1970), 'An investigation of the differences in measured intelligence between twins and single births', *Annals hum. Genet.*, vol. 34, pp. 11–20.

REED, E. W., and REED, S. C. (1965), *Mental Retardation: A Family Study*, Saunders.

RIFE, D. C. (1940), 'Handedness with special reference to twins', *Genetics*, vol. 25, pp. 178–86.

ROBINSON, W. P., and RACKSTRAW, S. J. (1967), 'Variations in mothers' answers to children's questions, as a function of social class, intelligence test scores and sex', *Sociology*, vol. 1, pp. 259–76.

ROSANOFF, A. J., HANDY, L. M., PLESSET, I. R., and BRISH, S. (1934), 'The etiology of so-called schizophrenic psychoses with special reference to their occurrence in twins', *Amer. J. Psychiat.*, vol. 91, pp. 247–86.

ROSANOFF, A. J., HANDY, L. M., and PLESSET, I. R. (1935), 'The etiology of manic-depressive syndromes with special reference to their occurrence in twins', *Amer. J. Psychiat.*, vol. 91, pp. 225–362.

ROSENTHAL, D. (1962), 'Problems of sampling and diagnosis in the major twin studies of schizophrenia', *J. psychiat. Res.*, vol. 1, pp. 116–34.

ROSENTHAL, D. (1968), 'The heredity-environment issue in schizophrenia', *J. psychiat. Res.*, vol. 6, supp. 1, pp. 413–28.

ROSENTHAL, D., and KETTY, S. (eds.), (1968), 'The transmission of schizophrenia', *J. psychiat. Res.*, vol. 6, supp. 1.

ROSENTHAL, D., WENDER, P., KETY, S., SCHULSINGER, F., WELNER, J., and OSTERGAARD, L. (1968), 'Schizophrenics' offspring in adoptive homes', *J. psychiat. Res.*, vol. 6, supp. 1, pp. 377–92.

RUTTER, M., KORN, S., and BIRCH, H. G. (1962), 'Genetic and environmental factors in the development of "primary reaction patterns" ', *Brit. J. soc. clin. Psychol.*, vol. 2, pp. 161–73.

SANDON, F. (1957), 'The relative numbers and abilities of some ten-year-old twins', *J. Roy. Statist. Soc.*, vol. 120, pp. 440–50.

SANDON, F. (1959), 'Twins in the school population', *Brit. J. statist. Psychol.*, vol. 12, pp. 133–8.

SCARR, S. (1966), 'Genetic factors in activity motivation', *Child Devel.*, vol. 37, pp. 663–73.

SCARR, S. (1968) 'Environmental bias in twin studies', in S. G. Vandenberg (ed.), *Progress in Human Behavior Genetics*, Johns Hopkins Press.

SCARR, S. (1969), 'Social introversion–extraversion as a heritable response', *Child Devel.*, vol. 40, pp. 823–32.

183 References

SCHAEFFER, W. S., and BAYLEY, N. (1963), 'Maternal behavior, child behavior and their intercorrelations from infancy through adolescence', *Monogrs. Soc. Res. child Devel.*, vol. 28, pp. 1–127.

SCHEINFELD, A. (1968), *Twins and Supertwins*, Chatto & Windus.

SCOTTISH COUNCIL FOR RESEARCH IN EDUCATION (1939), *The Intelligence of Scottish Children*, University of London Press.

SCOTTISH COUNCIL FOR RESEARCH IN EDUCATION (1949), *The Trend of Scottish Intelligence*, University of London Press.

SCOTTISH COUNCIL FOR RESEARCH IN EDUCATION (1953), *Social Implications of the 1947 Scottish Mental Survey*, University of London Press.

SHAFFER, H. R. (1965), 'Changes in developmental quotient under two conditions of separation', *Brit. J. soc. clin. Psychol*, vol. 4, pp. 39–46.

SHAFFER, H. R., and EMERSON, P. (1964), 'The development of social attachments in infancy', *Monogrs. Soc. Res. child Devel.*, vol. 29, (3).

SHIELDS, J. (1954), 'Personality differences and neurotic traits in normal school children', *Eugen. Rev.*, vol. 45, pp. 213–45.

SHIELDS, J. (1962), *Monozygotic Twins Brought Up Together and Apart*, Oxford University Press.

SHIELDS, J. (1968), 'Summary of the genetic evidence', *J. psychiat. Res.*, vol. 6, supp. 1, pp. 95–126.

SHIELDS, J., and SLATER, E. (1960), 'Heredity and psychological abnormality', in H. J. Eysenck (ed.), *Handbook of Abnormal Psychology*, Pitman.

SHIELDS, J., GOTTESMAN, I. I., and SLATER, E. (1967), 'Kallmann's 1946 schizophrenia twin study in the light of new information', *Acta psychiat. Scand.*, vol. 43, pp. 385–96.

SKODAK, M., and SKEELS, H. M. (1949), 'A final follow-up study of one hundred adopted children', *J. genet. Psychol.*, vol. 75, pp. 85–125.

SLATER, E. (1953), 'Psychotic and neurotic illnesses in twins', MRC Report, HMSO.

SLATER, E. (1961), 'Hysteria 311', *J. ment. Sci.*, vol. 197, pp. 359–81.

SLATER, E. (1962), 'Birth order and maternal age of homosexuals', *Lancet*, vol. 1, pp. 69–71.

SLATER, E. (1968), 'A review of earlier evidence on genetic factors in schizophrenia', *J. psychiat, Res.*, vol. 6, supp. 1, pp. 15–26.

SMITH, G. (1949), 'Psychological studies in twin differences', *Studia psychol. pedagog.*, vol. 3.

SMITH, G. (1953), 'Twin differences with respect to the Muller–Leyer illusion', Lunds Universitet Arrskrift N.F. Aud., vol. 50, pp. 1–27.

SMITH, S. M., and PENROSE, L. S. (1955), 'Monozygotic and dizygotic twin diagnosis', *Annals hum. Genet.*, vol. 19, pp. 273–89.

SPÄTH, J. (1860), 'Studien über Zwillingen', *Z. d. Wien. Gesellsch. D. Artze zu Wien*, vol. 16, pp. 225–41.

SPOCK, B. (1946), *Baby and Child Care*, originally published as *The Common Sense Book of Baby and Child Care*, Duell, Sloan & Pearce.

STABENAU, J. R., POLLIN, W., and ALLEN, M. (1970), 'Twin studies of schizophrenia and neurosis', *Seminars in Psychiatry*, vol. 2, pp. 65–74.

STRAYER, C. (1930), 'The relative efficacy of early and deferred vocabulary training studied by the method of co-twin control', *Genet. Psychol. Monogrs.*, vol. 8, pp. 209–319.

STRONG, S. J., and CORNEY, G. (1967), *The Placenta in Twin Pregnancy*, Pergamon.

STUMPFL, F. (1937), 'Untersuchungen an psychopathischen Zwillingen', *Z. Ges. Neurol. Psychiat.*, vol. 158, pp. 480–82.

TEASDALE, G. R., and KATZ, F. M. (1968), 'Psycholinguistic abilities of children from different ethnic and socio-economic backgrounds', *Aust. J. Psychol.*, vol. 20, pp. 155–9.

THOMAS, A., BIRCH, H. G., CHESS, S. A., HERTZIG, M., and KORN, S. (1964), *Behavoural Individuality in Early Childhood*, University of London Press.

THORNDIKE, E. L. (1905), 'Measurement of twins', *Arch. Phil., Psychol., sci. Methods*, vol. 1, pp. 1–64.

THURSTONE, T. G., THURSTONE, L. L., and STRANDKOV, H. H. (1955), *A Psychological Study of Twins*, University of North Carolina Press.

TIENARI, P. (1963), 'Psychiatric illness in identical twins', *Acta psychiat.*, supp. 171

TIENARI, P. (1968), 'Schizophrenia in monozygotic male twins', *J. psychiat. Res.*, vol. 6, supp. 1.

VANDENBERG, S. G. (1962), 'The hereditary abilities study: hereditary components in a psychological test battery', *Amer. J. hum. Genet.*, vol. 14, pp. 220–37.

VANDENBERG, S. G. (1965), 'Multivariate analysis of twin differences', in S. G. Vandenberg (ed.), *Methods and Goals in Human Behavior Genetics*, Academic Press.

VANDENBERG, S. G. (1966), 'The contribution of twin research to psychology', *Psychol. Bull.*, vol. 66, pp. 327–52.

VANDENBERG, S. G. (ed.), (1968a), *Progress in Human Behavior Genetics*, Johns Hopkins Press.

VANDENBERG, S. G. (1968b), 'The nature and nurture of intelligence', in D. C. Glass (ed.), *Genetics*, Rockefeller Press and Russell Sage Foundation.

VANDENBERG, S. G. (1969a), 'Human behavior and genetics: present status and suggestions for future research', *Merrill Palmer Q.*, vol. 15, pp. 121–54.

VANDENBERG, S. G. (1969b), 'A twin study of spatial ability', *Multivariate Behavior Res.*, vol. 4, pp. 273–94.

VANDENBERG, S. G., CLARK, P. J., and SAMUELS, I. (1965), 'Psychophysiological reactions of twins: heritability estimates of galvanic skin resistance, heart beat and breathing rates', *Eugen. Q.*, vol. 12, pp. 7–10.

VANDENBERG, S. G., and JOHNSON, R. C. (1968), 'Further evidence of the relation between age of separation and similarity in IQ among pairs of separated identical twins', in S. G. Vandenberg (ed.), *Progress in Human Behavior Genetics*, Johns Hopkins Press.

VENABLES, P. (1966), 'Psychophysiological aspects of schizophrenia', *Brit. J. med. Psychol.*, vol. 39, pp. 289–96.

VERNON, P. E. (1960), *Intelligence and Attainment Tests*, University of London Press.

VIGOTSKY, L. S. (1962), *Thought and Language*, Harvard University Press.

WALTER, G. (1969), 'The development of electrocerebral activity in children', in J. G. Howells (ed.), *Modern Perspectives in International Child Psychiatry*, Oliver & Boyd.

WARBURTON, F. W., FITZPATRICK, T., WARD, J., and RITCHIE, M. (1970), 'Some problems in the construction of intelligence tests', in P. Mittler (ed.), *Psychological Assessment of Mental and Physical Handicaps*, Methuen.

WEAVER, S. J., and WEAVER, A. (1967), 'Psycholinguistic abilities of culturally deprived Negro children', *Amer. J. ment. Deficiency*, vol. 72, pp. 190–97.

WICTORIN, M. (1952), *Bidrag till Raknedfardighetens Psykologi, en Twilling-undersokning*, Elanders, Sweden.

WILDE, G. J. S. (1964), 'Inheritance of personality traits', *Acta Psychol.*, vol. 22, pp. 37–51.

WILDER, T. (1941), *The Bridge of San Luis Rey*, Penguin Books.

WILLERMAN, L., and CHURCHILL, J. A. (1967), 'Intelligence and birth weight in identical twins', *Child Devel.*, vol. 38, pp. 623–9.

WINGFIELD, A. H. (1928), *Twins and Orphans: The Inheritance of Intelligence*, Dent.

WISEMAN, S. (1964), *Education and Environment*, Manchester University Press.

WISEMAN, S. (1966), 'Environmental and innate factors and educational attainment', in J. E. Meades and A. S. Parkes (eds.), *Genetic and Environmental Factors in Human Ability*, Oliver & Boyd.

WISEMAN, S. (1967), 'The Manchester Survey' in The Plowden Report, *Children and their Primary Schools*, Central Advisory Council for Education, Appendix 9, HMSO.

WITHERSPOON, R. L. (1965), 'Selected areas of development of twins in relation to zygosity', in S. G. Vandenberg (ed.), *Methods and Goals in Human Behavior Genetics*, Academic Press.

WITTENBORN, J. R. (1965), 'Depression', in B. Wolman (ed.), *Handbook of Clinical Psychology*, McGraw-Hill.

WOOLF, L. I., GRIFFITHS, R., MONTCRIEFF, A., COATES, S., and DILLSTONE, F. (1958), 'Dietary treatment of phenylketonuria', *Arch. Dis. Child.*, vol. 33, p. 31.

WORLD HEALTH ORGANIZATION (1966), 'The use of twins in epidemiological studies', *Acta Genet. Med. Gemellog.*, vol. 15, pp. 109–28.

WYNNE, L. C. (1968), 'Methodological and conceptual issues in the study of schizophrenics and their families', *J. psychiat. Res.*, vol. 6, supp. 1, pp. 185–200.

ZAZZO, R. (1960), *Les Jumeaux: Le Couple et la Personne*, Presses Universitaires de France.

Index